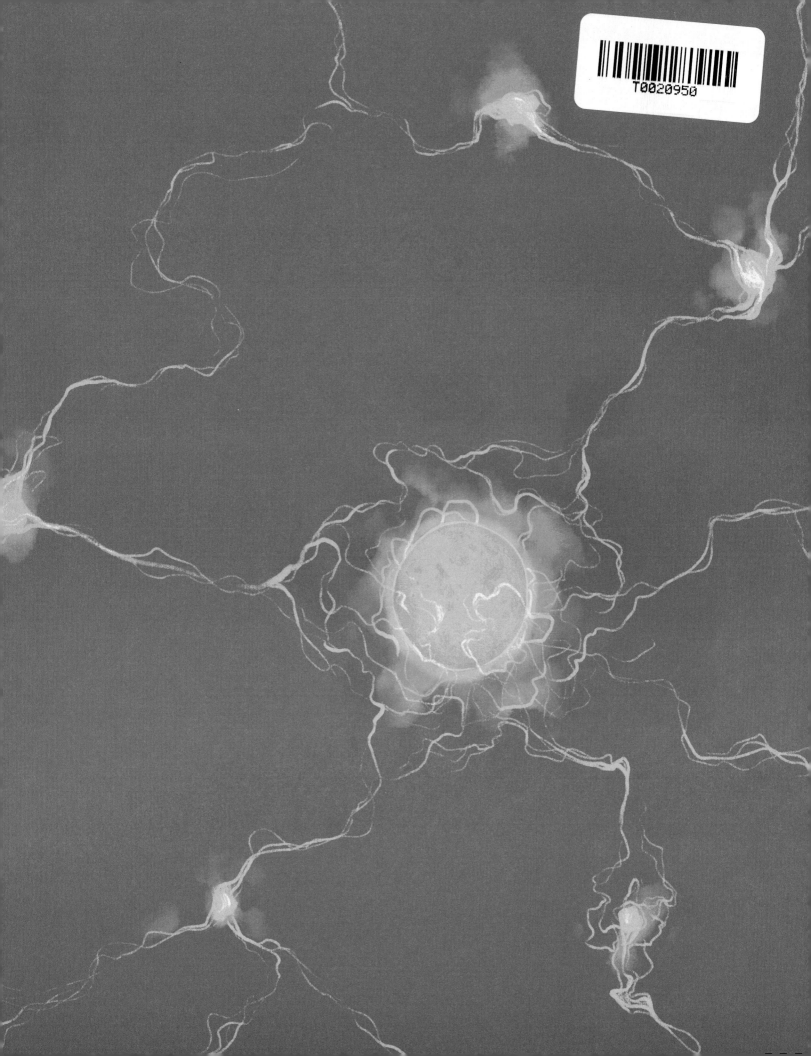

THE STORY OF PLANET EARTH

From Stardust to the Modern World

THE STORY OF PLANET EARTH

From Stardust to the Modern World

Written by
Anne Rooney

Illustrated by
Margarida Esteves

ARCTURUS

ARCTURUS

This edition published in 2022
by Arcturus Publishing Limited
26/27 Bickels Yard, 151–153 Bermondsey Street,
London SE1 3HA

Copyright © Arcturus Holdings Limited

Author: Anne Rooney
Illustrator: Margarida Esteves
Designer: Sally Bond
Design Manager: Jessica Holliland
Editor: Donna Gregory
Editorial Manager: Joe Harris

ISBN: 978-1-83940-614-0
CH007800NT
Supplier 42, Date 0821, Print run 11628

Printed in Singapore

CONTENTS

WELCOME TO PLANET EARTH

We live on a small planet, going around a medium-sized star, in a fairly average spiral galaxy whirling through the universe. Although it's only a speck in the vastness of space, everything we know is rooted here. Our home, Earth, is the only place we know that life exists, and it's the only planet whose history we can trace.

Once upon a time ...

For thousands of years, people have wondered how Earth came into being and what causes strange and frightening events like earthquakes and volcanic eruptions. In the past, people made up stories to explain these mysteries. The stories became myths, legends, and religions.

Many cultures have creation stories to explain Earth's origins. A Cherokee myth, rooted in the landscape of North America, claims that Earth was created at a time when there was only water and sky. All the animals lived in the sky realm, known as Gälûñ'läti. The sacred Little Water Beetle, Dayuni'si, came down to see what was below the water. It brought up mud, which expanded to make the world. Other animals wanted to explore, but the buzzard flew down first to check whether the soil was dry. His giant wings brushed against the smooth surface of the damp soil, forming mountains and valleys. When the surface dried, the other animals settled on land. It was entirely dark, so they set the Sun in the sky, and set the Sun in the sky to light and warm Earth.

Chinese and Indian myths describe a world supported by several elephants standing on the back of a turtle. When one of the animals moves, the Earth trembles and shakes, producing the terrifying earthquakes that are common in parts of China and India.

Disasters tamed by stories
People also explained frightening and destructive natural events, such as earthquakes and floods, with fantastic stories. Finding a cause helped them deal with the seemingly senseless death and destruction these events brought.

In the Pacific North West, traditional stories speak of a struggle between a whale and a large bird—the Thunderbird— that causes the ground to shake and the sea to flood the land. Many cultures have explained volcanic eruptions in terms of the actions of supernatural beings, such as the godess Pele in Hawai'i or the devil Guayota among the Guanche of Tenerife.

A PLANET TO CALL HOME

Today, we use science to explain how Earth works, and to explore the history of our planet. We know it is one of eight spherical planets moving around the Sun. We know how old it is and how it formed, how the land, sea, and air came about, and how living things interact with the planet.

Biosphere

Lithosphere

North America

Europe

Asia

Pacific
Ocean

Africa

Indian
Ocean

South
America

Atlantic
Ocean

Australia

warm surface flow

cool subsurface flow

Endless change

Earth is constantly changing.
The landscape of the planet today has
developed over billions of years. The current map of land, oceans, islands, and ice caps
is just a snapshot in Earth's history. Things have been arranged differently in the past
and will be again in the future. The sea and land move around, mountains rise and fall,
the atmosphere changes, and the climate shifts from hot to cold and back again. It's a
dynamic system in which all the parts work together, each one changing the others.

Over a shorter timescale, from days and weeks to centuries, Earth's resources are naturally recycled and renewed. The water of the oceans flows around the world, and moves between the top and bottom of the sea in a cycle that takes around 2,000 years, but the tides ebb and flow each day.

A world of spheres

Scientists divide Earth into the **lithosphere** (rocks), the **hydrosphere** (water—the oceans, seas, lakes, rivers, and ice), the **atmosphere** (air), and the **biosphere** (living things). These are all interconnected. Chemicals cycle through rock, water, air, and living things again and again. Life is affected by the climate, and affects it in turn. And although it might seem unlikely, living things even affect the rocks. It's a complex web, held in a fragile balance. It has been tippped into extreme conditions in the past, and no doubt will be again.

Atmosphere

Hydrosphere

Lithosphere

The currents of air in the atmosphere follow their own cycles. The weather and ocean currents follow complex patterns that we have still not fully unpicked—which is why the weather forecast is often wrong!

The more scientists investigate, the more we learn about how our planet has grown and how it works. Earth's story is a fascinating saga of building a beautiful system that supports us, and all other living things. It's far from over—the Sun is only about halfway through its life, so a lot lies ahead for our planet.

Tornado

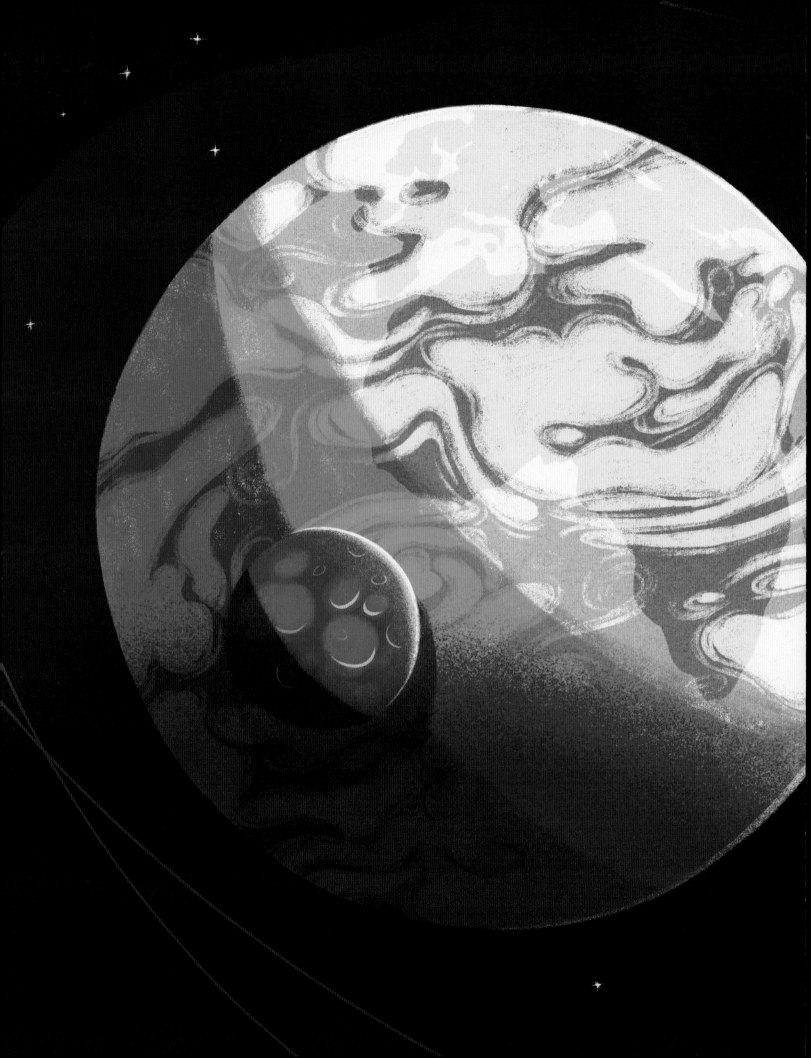

A WORLD FROM THE STARS

Our planet and its seven companions formed from a cloud of matter whirling around the new Sun. As the specks of rock dust and ice hurtled through space, they crashed into each other, some sticking together and some smashing apart. Clumps grew larger and larger until, after thousands of years, one of the rockier lumps became the start of Earth. Four and a half billion years later, our planet is teeming with life, active both at its surface and deep within. It is still whizzing around the

FROM DARKNESS TO LIGHT

Our Earth and even the Sun are late arrivals on the cosmic scene. The universe is far older than the solar system. It probably began 13.8 billion years ago with the "Big Bang" when space-time burst into existence as an infinitely tiny, infinitely hot and infinitely dense point. There was nothing recognizable in this baby universe—no stars, matter, or even space.

Really big, really fast

Instantly, the tiny universe expanded at unimaginable speed. It was as if a single grain of rice grew to be 1,000 times as long as the entire galaxy—in less than a second! It was so tiny to start with, that even after all that growth it was still smaller than an orange.

The universe is all there is. There is nothing outside it (as far as we know), not even empty space. This has always been true, so even when the universe was really tiny, it was all that existed, and there was nothing outside it.

GRAVITY

Gravity works between objects that have mass, drawing them toward each other. You are held on Earth by Earth's gravity, but you also exert a

Holding on

The universe continued to grow, though not as quickly, and to cool. After a few minutes, the first matter came into being. This matter was the nuclei (middles) of atoms of the gases hydrogen and helium. Gravity made the new matter clump together. Areas where, randomly, there was a little more gas than elsewhere attracted more and more gas. After 100 million years, some areas had so much gas squashed together that the intense gravity at the middle crushed the nuclei, creating the first stars. They began to pour light and other types of energy into space.

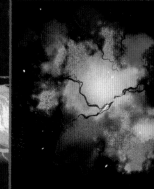

Nebula collapse
A huge cloud (nebula) of concentrated gas collapses inward.

Protostar
The middle of the collapsing nebula begins to glow as it gets hotter and hotter.

Outflow
Jets of super-heated gas pour from the poles of the protostar.

A star starts!
Finally, the middle is so dense it starts to fuse hydrogen, becoming a star.

Stars are energy factories

In a star, hydrogen is crushed together under the immense pressure created by gravity. There is so little space that the hydrogen nuclei fuse and make helium nuclei. It takes four hydrogen nuclei to make a helium nucleus, but one helium nucleus takes up less space than the four hydrogen nuclei. Energy is released as the nuclei fuse, and this is the heat and light we get from the Sun.

A star like the Sun has so much hydrogen inside that it can "burn" for billions of years. Our Sun is only in the middle of its life and will produce energy for another four billion years.

MAKING THE MATERIALS FOR PLANET-BUILDING

The first stars lived fast and furious lives and died young. After them came generations of new stars, including—eventually—our own Sun.

Supernova

Matter is hurled outward.

Inside a star

Core

Making metals

Stars create helium until they start to run out of hydrogen. Then the middle of the star starts to fuse the helium to make heavier chemical elements, such as carbon and oxygen. (Elements are the fundamental ingredients of all other chemicals.) The heaviest element a star can make in this way is iron. The process of creating elements up to the weight of iron releases energy, producing the star's light and heat. To make an element heavier than iron, extra energy would be needed to fuse nuclei, so this doesn't happen.

Out with a bang

The energy escaping from an active star produces an outward pressure. This balances gravity pulling inward, so the star stays the same size. Once a large star has a core of iron, it can no longer produce energy. The pull of gravity makes it collapse inward in a catastrophic crash. But there is no space in the middle, so it all bounces back out in a massive explosion called a supernova. This has so much energy it fuses iron to form heavier elements, such as gold and platinum. The supernova blasts all the elements made in the star and its destruction out to space.

CHEMICAL ELEMENTS

There are 98 naturally occurring chemical elements, all made in stars or supernovas. Each has a different design of atom. All other chemicals in the universe are made by combining the elements, which form the building-blocks of all matter.

Now you see it ...

Supernovas make the largest explosions in the universe. The explosion itself lasts only seconds, but pours out more energy than the star has released in its entire life. The remains of an exploded star spread out into space in an ever-growing and thinning cloud of material. The last supernova in our galaxy, in 1604, was visible in Earth's sky even in daylight, and shone for months. The remains of it can still be seen with a telescope.

Remnant of a supernova

Get set for planets

The extra elements hurled out into space can be swept up in the next set of forming stars. But stars only need hydrogen to burn—they can't use the extra material. Instead, it can be used to make planets.

FROM DISK TO GLOBE

For billions of years, stars formed and died, adding more and more chemical ingredients to the cosmic soup. They clustered into massive galaxies that included large and small stars. About 4.6 billion years ago, in one arm of the spiral galaxy we call the Milky Way, our own cloud of hot gas and dust formed.

Sun

SOLID, LIQUID, GAS

Any substance can exist as a solid, a liquid, or a gas, depending on the pressure and temperature. We are used to water in all three forms—as ice (solid), water (liquid), and as water droplets in the air (gas). The state depends on how the particles are spaced out.

Making a solar system

Most material in the cloud was pulled to the middle where it was under such pressure it began to fuse hydrogen, lighting up a star—our Sun—just as billions of stars had lit up before it. Extra material whirling around the new Sun flattened into a disk-shaped cloud. This included all the elements that had been thrown out of dying stars over billions of years. From this, the planets, moons, and asteroids of the solar system would form.

Hot and cold

Very close to the Sun it's so hot that substances that are solid on Earth exist as gases. Further from the Sun, space grows cooler and cooler. Materials with a high melting point—such as rock and metal—freeze close to the Sun and form dust in the spinning cloud. Further out, matter that is liquid or even gas on Earth can freeze into solid specks.

Billions of years ago, as particles collided, they formed clumps and lumps. Over time, these grew into larger and larger lumps as they combined in collisions—a process called accretion. Some of these lumps became the first baby protoplanets, and eventually the planets we know today. In just five million years, Earth grew from dust to an early planet. That might sound like a long time, but in the life of stars and planets, it's no time at all.

ACCRETION

Accreting lumps

Protoplanet

Gravity pulls the lumps together.

"frost line"

Hydrogen-helium gas nebula

Sun

Accreting rock-ice planetesimals

Accreting rocky planetesimals

Lumps and chunks continued to crash into and be added to accreting planetesimals.

Rocky planets, gassy planets

Rocky planets like Earth formed closest to the Sun. Matter with a lower freezing point formed lumps further out, making the gas planets like Jupiter. Earth is inside the "frost line"—an imaginary line around the Sun that marks the point at which chemicals such as water and methane freeze. Each substance has its own more precise frost line.

Surface of a protoplanet

HOT ROCKS!

Gravity pulls on each part of a forming planet equally, so the matter forms into a sphere (ball shape). Originally, the matter that made up the Earth was evenly distributed, as the planet was made from lots of lumps of similar substances gathered together. As Earth grew, that changed.

Protoplanet

Start of protoplanetary melting

The interior is hot and mostly molten

Metals move toward the core

Core

Rivulets of molten metal creep through rock.

Creeping metals

Gravity pulled the heaviest matter—metals such as iron and nickel—toward the middle of the Earth. Molten metal seeped between grains of rock as water seeps through coffee in a filter. Tiny rivers of liquid metal oozed through the rock, threading their way toward Earth's core.

Metals moving to the middle heated Earth more and more, eventually making it hot enough to melt rock. Now, Earth has a core of heavy metal, and a thick coat of lighter, semi-molten rock. Water and gases are lightest of all, and stay near the surface.

Molten in the middle

Gravity pulls material toward the middle of Earth, creating great pressure, and putting material under pressure heats it up. Radioactive materials in Earth change naturally over time, releasing heat as they do so. So, as Earth formed, the heat produced by accretion—the clumping together of all the bits of rock, metal, and ice to make a planet—and radioactivity was enough to melt metal. The heat, most intense in the middle, spread through the planet, and still does. Early Earth began to melt from the middle, making it easier for materials in it to move around.

A crispy crust

Although Earth was heated from the middle, the outside was (and is) cooled by space. The surface hardened to a crust of dark, hard rock. Despite this, it was still frequently broken by asteroids smashing into it, breaking and melting the crust. Hot magma (semi-molten rock) broke through the crust from beneath and melted the rocky surface, too. Magma now forms a layer of hot, semi-molten rock called the mantle. When magma comes out of volcanoes, it's called lava.

Hard crust

Mantle

Very hot metallic core

Early Earth

MAKING A MOON

Earth suffered a terrible accident early in its life—it had a collision with another small planet about the size of Mars. This planet has been named Theia; it was completely destroyed in the collision. Earth came out of the crash with a lot of damage—and a brand new Moon.

Theia

Earth

The short life of planet Theia

Like Earth, Theia formed from small chunks of rock and dust crashing together in space. Unfortunately, Theia's orbit around the Sun crossed the path of Earth's orbit. Sooner or later, a collision was bound to happen. Within about 100 million years of the formation of the solar system, around 4.5–4.4 billion years ago, the crash came. It was so violent that rock from both planets was instantly heated to its boiling point and vaporized into a cloud. A large part of Earth was blasted into space and Theia was smashed apart. Much or all of Earth's surface was melted, perhaps to a depth of several thousand miles.

Looking inside

Although the new Moon was made of a mix of Earth and Theia, the material from Earth was mostly from the rocky mantle. As a result, the Moon has only a small metal core that probably came from Theia. Unlike Earth, the Moon has no liquid water on its surface, and no atmosphere.

HOW DO WE KNOW?

The Apollo missions to the Moon in the 1960s and 1970s collected pieces of Moon rock that scientists have examined. These pieces show that Moon rock is similar to rock on Earth, but not exactly the same. The Moon could be anything from half to nine-tenths material from Theia, the rest coming from Earth.

Earth

0° axis

Theia

From rock cloud to Moon

As the rock gas cooled, it formed small chunks of solid rock. Some of these fell back to Earth and were mixed into the molten surface, becoming part of the planet as it slowly cooled and solidified again. But much of the rock stayed in orbit around Earth. The cloud of debris circled Earth, the little chunks colliding and accreting all over again. Eventually, all the chunks were swept up into a single body, which became the Moon. It had enough mass to become round as gravity pulled it together. The collision tipped Earth sideways, so that its axis is no longer upright.

Theia crashes into Earth

Debris

Axis now 23°

Debris orbits Earth

Debris forms the Moon

Earth becomes round again under gravity

SETTLING DOWN

The Moon and Earth settled into a stable state, with the Moon in orbit around Earth. Earth had to adjust, as the collision with Theia caused immense damage to the newly formed planet.

Moving apart

The Moon started out much closer to Earth than it is now, at only 24,000–32,000 km (15,000–20,000 mi) away. It would have looked 15 times as big in the sky as it does now, and would have glowed red from its molten-rock surface. The Moon is now 384,400 km (238,855 mi) away—a distance that is 30 times the diameter of Earth. It's still drifting further from Earth, moving away at a rate of 3.8 cm (1.5 in) a year.

WOBBLY PLANET

Earth is not entirely stable on its feet—or axis. In fact, it wobbles in a 41,000-year cycle so that the North and South poles point toward slightly different parts of the sky on this cycle. The result is that the "North" star is not always due north, and sometimes there is no pole star. There is currently no southern pole star.

Always the same

The Moon has settled into an orbit that makes it tidally locked with Earth. This means that the same side of the Moon always faces Earth. The far side of the Moon was first seen in 1959, when it was photographed from space by *Luna 3*. The Moon turns on its own axis once every 27 days, making one "Moon day" 27.3 Earth-days long. This is the same time as the duration of its orbit around Earth.

Getting back on track

The semi-molten Earth was pulled back into a sphere by gravity, and its surface slowly hardened again as it cooled. But Earth had been pushed over in its collision with Theia. The North and South poles had originally been top and bottom, but the collision pushed the planet off its vertical axis, so that even now it tilts at an angle of 23 degrees. This tilt gives Earth its seasons—the hemisphere (half) that is tilted toward the Sun has longer days and so gets warmer—this is summer. The half that is tilted away is cooler, so when it's summer in the northern hemisphere, it's winter in the southern hemisphere, and vice versa.

Autumn (Fall)/
Spring

Winter

Summer

SUN

Summer

Winter

23° tilt

Spring/Autumn (Fall)

DELIVERIES FROM SPACE

Although lots of material in the early solar system was gathered up into the forming planets, quite a lot was left over. This circled the Sun in lumps and clumps, occasionally colliding with other things. There are still a lot of leftover lumps floating around.

Relics from the birth of the solar system

Asteroids are lumps of rock, dust and ice that have not changed in 4.5 billion years. From them, we can learn about the material from which the solar system formed. Those nearest the Sun, in the Asteroid Belt, are made mostly of rock, mixed with some ice. Those furthest away from the Sun, in the Kuiper Belt, contain more ice and less rock dust. They appear as comets if they come close enough to the Sun, as the heat melts the ice and produces a streaming, glowing tail.

Smashing times

Asteroids and smaller meteoroids sometimes crash into each other, or into planets or moons. They have always done so, and still do. Collisions were more frequent in the past because there were more asteroids—some have since been destroyed in these crashes. We can see from the cratered surface of the Moon how many strikes there have been. Some craters have been filled in with lava from beneath, but many are still visible, and many contain smaller craters.

Craters on the Moon

Asteroids

Earth has been hit by just as many asteroids, but the surface changes too quickly for craters to remain. There has never again been a collision as catastrophic as that which created the Moon. Early in Earth's history, crashing asteroids melted parts of the planet's surface and were then absorbed into the crust and mantle. They brought extra material to Earth, including rock, gases and water.

TUNGANUSKA METEOR

In 1908, an explosion above Tunganuska in Russia flattened about 80 million trees over an area of 2,000 square km (772 square mi). The blast was probably caused by an asteroid about 100 m (328 ft) across burning up in the atmosphere. It exploded with the force of several hundred atomic bombs. Luckily, it happened over an uninhabited area.

Comet

ROUND AND ROUND

You might feel as though you are standing still on Earth, but you're actually whizzing through space at a phenomenal speed. Earth goes around the Sun, the whole galaxy rotates around its own midpoint, and the Milky Way itself is rushing through space.

SUN

Earth

Moon

A push and a shove

The matter that went on to make up Earth was all whirling around the Sun in the same direction—counterclockwise. As the parts came together, the growing planet carried on moving in the same direction. Chunks colliding with the growing Earth gave it a shove, setting the early Earth spinning, again in the same direction.

Marking time

Earth turns on its axis every 24 hours, making a day and a night. When your side of Earth faces the Sun, it's daytime, and when it faces the darkness of space, it's nighttime.

Earth goes around the Sun once a year. Currently, a year is 365 ¼ days long.

Milky Way galaxy midpoint

Whizzing through space

Each spot on Earth makes a full turn each day, but a place on the equator has to move further, and so travels more quickly, than places near the poles. A spot on the equator moves at 1,670 km/h (1,037 mph).

Earth travels around the Sun at an average speed of 107,000 km/h (67,000 mph). The entire solar system orbits the middle of the Milky Way over 226 million years at a speed of 217 km/second (134 mi/second), or 781,200 km/h (485,415 mph). And the Milky Way is hurtling through space at 630 km/second (391 mi/second), or 2,268,000 km/h (1,409,269 mph).

DAYS OF THE DEAD

For dinosaurs like T. rex, the days were about 23.5 hours long; earlier dinosaurs such as Stegosaurus enjoyed 23 hour days, and early sponges 600 million years ago had a day of just 21 hours—but a year was the same length. A Stegosaurus would need to wait 381 days for its birthday; an ancient sponge would have had a birthday every 417 days.

The days are getting longer

A day has not always been 24 hours long. When the Moon formed, Earth was spinning much faster on its axis—days were just two or three hours long. The brand-new Moon went around Earth in about five hours. The pull of the Moon's gravity has gradually slowed Earth's rotation.

Earth is still slowing, but you won't notice any change. A day increases by only 1/500th of a second every century, so it will take 50,000 years to lengthen by just one second.

THE MAKING OF A PLANET

As Earth settled into its orbit around the Sun, with its companion Moon going around it, it set about becoming the planet we know. Over the next hundred million years or so it would acquire a solid surface of rock, oceans of salt water, and a gassy atmosphere above. It was a dynamic, ever-changing, new planet that would soon be ready for the greatest of changes—the appearance of living things. First, it needed to settle from its chaotic and turbulent origins.

INGREDIENTS FOR A PLANET

All matter is made from 98 naturally occurring chemical elements.
They are the fundamental ingredients of all other chemicals.
Ten of the natural elements are very rare, or exist
only briefly, so most matter is made of just
88 elements. A further 20 elements
have been made in laboratories,
but are not found in nature.

Atoms and molecules

An atom is the smallest possible
particle of a substance. Each
element has a distinct design of
atom that is different from all other
elements. Most types of atom can
combine with other atoms in set
ways. When two or more atoms bond
together they make a molecule.

Atom

Molecules

Compound

Mixture

Some atoms generally pair up with others of the same type to
make a simple molecule. For example, hydrogen, nitrogen, and
oxygen all pair up in this way, making molecules that have two
hydrogen atoms, two nitrogen atoms, or two oxygen atoms.
These are still elements as they contain only one type of atom.

When atoms of different elements bond to
make a molecule, the new substance is a
compound. The compound is completely different
from the elements in it. For example, water is
made of hydrogen and oxygen. These are gases
at room temperature, but water is a liquid.
Compounds can be broken apart (sometimes
with difficulty) to return the original elements.
A mixture has different chemicals but they
are not bonded.

WHAT EARTH'S MADE OF

By weight, Earth is nearly a third iron and nearly a third oxygen. Most of the rest is silicon and magnesium, with 9 percent made up of other elements. Different elements dominate different layers. The crust (outside) is mostly silicate rock, made of silicon and oxygen, but the core is mostly iron and nickel. The core makes up about a third of the planet's total mass.

STATES OF MATTER

Solid

Liquid

Gas

In a solid, particles move very little and are held close together in a fixed shape.

In a liquid, particles are further apart and can move more freely. A spilled liquid quickly spreads out.

In a gas, particles are widely spaced and move freely. A gas rapidly fills the available space.

Mix it up

A mixture is a physical mix of elements or compounds. The particles of the substances don't bond together. A mix of iron filings and flakes of copper is a mixture of elements. A mix of salt and sand is a mixture of compounds. You can separate iron filings from copper flakes with a magnet, and separate salt and sand by adding hot water to dissolve the salt, then straining out the sand.

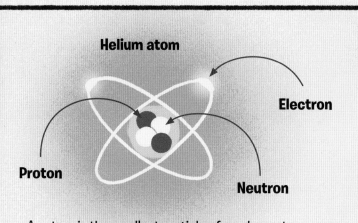

Helium atom

Electron

Proton

Neutron

An atom is the smallest particle of an element.

Substances can be elements, compounds, or mixtures.

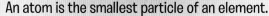

Gold nugget
element

Water
compound

Milk
a mixture of different compounds

SOLID LAND

Early in Earth's history, the core was hotter than it is now. Heat was left over from accretion, produced by friction as material sank inward, and from the collision with Theia. More heat was added by the radioactive decay of elements in the core (see pages 44–45). Earth is still very hot inside.

Liquid and solid rock

Over time, Earth slowly lost heat to space. The crust, exposed to freezing cold space, began to solidify early.

Rocks of different types melt at different temperatures. The first rocks to harden at Earth's surface would have been those with the highest melting point. Rocks also have different densities. Density is a measure of mass relative to volume. A dense substance is heavier than the same volume of a less dense substance—so stone is denser than wood, for example. The least dense types of rock floated to the surface, to the top of Earth's magma ocean, where they could cool.

Cool rock is more dense than hot rock, though, so some of the floating rock would then sink and remelt. There was a constant recycling of rock as cooler rock sank back into the magma ocean, heated up, melted, and rose again. Only the lightest bits of hardened rock stayed floating on top of the hot magma.

Ice floats because it is less dense than water.

OLDEST ROCKS

The first rocks to harden included crystals of zircon, which melts at about 2,550°C (4,600°F). A few crystals of zircon are all that's left of these first bits of Earth's crust. The oldest formed 4.4 billion years ago and have been found in Australia.

Islands in a sea of molten rock

Around four billion years ago, Earth had cooled enough for some slabs of rock to stay floating as islands above the magma. They moved around slowly, occasionally colliding and sticking together. Where more rock solidified between them, it glued them together. These growing patches of lasting rock became cratons, the roots of later continents. New rock also cooled and hardened under the cratons, making them thicker—cratons have deep keels or roots that go hundreds of miles into the mantle. But it seems that these islands of rock never grew very large. Less than a tenth of current continental rock consists of cratons formed more than three billion years ago.

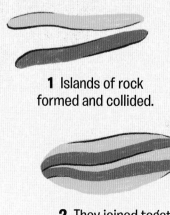

1 Islands of rock formed and collided.

2 They joined together in larger blocks.

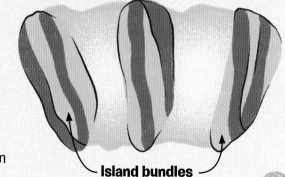

3 Primitive continents formed from groups of these blocks combining.

Island bundles

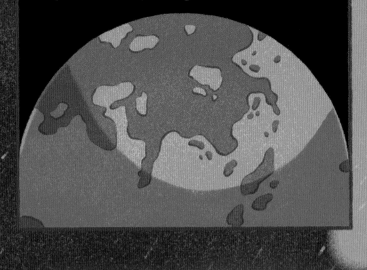

Early Earth developed large oceans of water.

A MILLION-YEAR RAINSTORM

Slowly, Earth was transformed from seething oceans of hot magma into a watery planet, its vast ocean dotted with growing islands of rock. Possibly by 4.2 billion years ago, and certainly by 3.8 billion years ago, Earth was a world of water.

Water from within

Earth's magma contains a mix of gases, including vaporized water and carbon dioxide. These had been clinging to the surface of the dust, lumps and chunks that accreted to form the planet. When the parts melted, the gases were trapped and dissolved in the hot molten rock. More arrived on asteroids that plunged into the forming planet. As hot magma rose to the surface, these gases escaped, like bubbles rising in boiling water or soup.

In and out

Right from the start, the oceans had tides. Tides are caused largely by the Moon's gravity. Because the Moon was closer to Earth, the tides were much stronger in the early ocean than they are today.

It tends to pile up in two bulges at Earth's "waist," one on the side nearest the Moon, and one on the opposite side, along an imaginary line drawn between the Moon and Earth. Earth turns beneath the bulges of water, each region falling under first one watery bulge and then the other. This gives two high tides each day.

The water of the oceans is pulled from the poles toward the equator where the Moon traces its path around Earth.

Tidal bulge

Pull from the Moon

MOON

EARTH

The Sun's gravity adds to the tides. When the Sun and Moon are lined up, there are extra-strong tides. When they are on opposite sides of Earth, the Sun cancels out some of the Moon's effect, making weaker tides.

Ocean world

At first, the water was a gas, but as it cooled, it condensed into clouds and fell as rain. When it fell onto scalding magma, it hissed, boiled and evaporated again, but when it fell onto cooler rock it lay in puddles and pools. It filled the craters made by crashing asteroids and spilled over all the cooling rock. Millions of years of constant rain eventually covered the surface of Earth with the oceans we have today.

THE SALTY SEA

The sea became salty early on. Chemicals dissolved from rocks by acidic rain and seawater collected in the ocean. They included the sodium and chlorine of salt. Now, plants and animals remove salt at about the same rate as it's added, so the ocean doesn't become saltier.

UNBREATHABLE AIRS

Water was not the only gas to escape from the magma. There was also a lot of carbon dioxide. These made Earth's atmosphere—but it wasn't the first atmosphere Earth had. The early atmospheres were nothing like our current air, and we couldn't have breathed them.

Here today, gone tomorrow

The very first atmosphere consisted of the gases hydrogen and helium that make up the Sun and the gas planets Jupiter and Saturn. This first atmosphere lay in a thin blanket over Earth's molten surface while the Sun was still powering up. But hydrogen and helium are very light gases. Before Earth's core had formed, these gases were pulled away by the solar wind—a stream of charged particles coming from the Sun—and were lost to space.

Moon

Trying again

The second atmosphere came from within, bubbling up from gases dissolved in the magma and released by chemical reactions in it. The new atmosphere was mostly vaporized water and carbon dioxide, with smaller portions of other gases such as ammonia, and methane. As the water condensed and fell as rain, most of what was left was carbon dioxide. The atmospheres of Venus and Mars today are rich in carbon dioxide and might be like that of early Earth.

Gases and water from within Earth still pour out of erupting volcanoes. Hardened lumps of lava are often light because they are full of holes, with a sponge-like texture. These holes were once bubbles of gas that have now escaped into the atmosphere.

A change of air

The very first living things to appear on Earth were a type of microbe called methanogens. They produced the gas methane—a compound of carbon and hydrogen—which they made by breaking down some of the carbon dioxide in the atmosphere. Methane is a powerful greenhouse gas, so adding methane to the air helped to keep Earth warm.

BLUE SKY THINKING

We don't know exactly what early Earth looked like. Many pictures show the sky tinged orange. A combination of dust in the atmosphere, clouds carrying yellow particles of sulfur, and clouds reflecting the orange and red of flowing lava might well have made the sky look yellowy orange. On a clear, eruption-free day, the sky could have been blue, as it is now.

LYING IN LAYERS

With a gassy atmosphere above a surface of water and rock, Earth had achieved the basic form it has now. Inside, it had separated into layers, with a metal core surrounded by a thick mantle of magma.

Atmosphere

Crust

Upper mantle

Mantle

Outer core

Inner core

A thin crust

We live on Earth's crust—the thin layer of rock, some flooded with water, that forms its surface. The crust is not stable and stationary, but is moved and changed by what happens beneath.

The crust is thinnest under the oceans, at just 5 km (3 mi) in some places. It is thickest under mountains, where it can reach 70 km (43.5 mi). What the crust is made of varies, with different types of rock in different places. Continental crust (land) contains a lot of granite, but oceanic crust (under the sea) is largely basalt.

Hot rock

Beneath the crust, the mantle is a layer of magma 2,900 km (1,800 mi) thick. It makes up more than 80 percent of Earth's volume. This hot rock moves very slowly, like road tar or a creeping glacier. Because Earth is hottest at the core, the lower part of the mantle is hotter than the top. Hot rock slowly rises from the bottom, while denser, colder rock falls downward to replace it. That in turn heats up and starts to rise, while the rock that has moved toward the surface cools and sinks down again in an unending cycle.

This happens very slowly as the magma is so thick. It takes millions of years for any bit of magma to make a full cycle of heating and cooling, rising and falling. The movement of the magma makes convection cells in the mantle. As magma near the top of the mantle moves, it carries parts of the crust with it, shifting it large distances over very long periods of time.

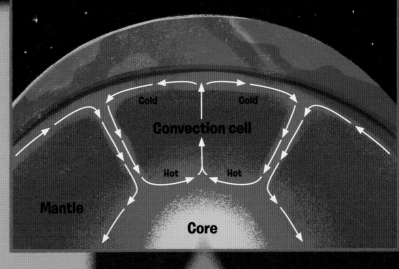

Cold   Cold
Convection cell
Hot   Hot
Mantle
Core

Deep inside

Below the mantle lies the core, made mostly of iron and nickel. The outer core is 2,400 km (1,500 mi) thick. It is liquid, and has its own convection currents. The inner core is solid. Even though it's extremely hot, the pressure is so great that the atoms can't move. There is possibly even an inner-inner core.

SEE FOR YOURSELF

CONVECTION CURRENTS

If you watch peas cooking in a pan of boiling water, you will notice they rise and fall with the hot water. The peas are carried by the convection currents in the water.

Earth's crust is a very thin outer layer—like the peel on an apple.

Cold   Cold
Hot   Hot

Convection cell

BUILDING ROCK

In Earth's early days, there were no large rocky areas above sea level, like modern continents. Rock was recycled quickly and slabs of rock moved around, probably more rapidly than now, dragged by the magma churning beneath.

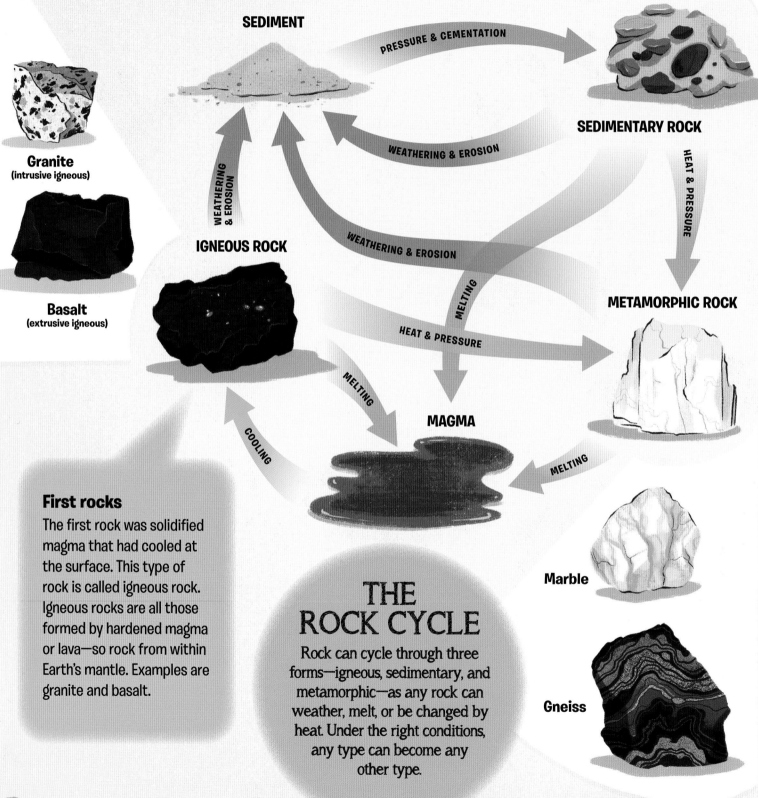

Granite
(intrusive igneous)

Basalt
(extrusive igneous)

SEDIMENT

PRESSURE & CEMENTATION

SEDIMENTARY ROCK

WEATHERING & EROSION

WEATHERING & EROSION

HEAT & PRESSURE

IGNEOUS ROCK

WEATHERING & EROSION

METAMORPHIC ROCK

MELTING

HEAT & PRESSURE

MELTING

COOLING

MAGMA

MELTING

Marble

Gneiss

First rocks

The first rock was solidified magma that had cooled at the surface. This type of rock is called igneous rock. Igneous rocks are all those formed by hardened magma or lava—so rock from within Earth's mantle. Examples are granite and basalt.

THE ROCK CYCLE

Rock can cycle through three forms—igneous, sedimentary, and metamorphic—as any rock can weather, melt, or be changed by heat. Under the right conditions, any type can become any other type.

sandstone

Worn away

Rock exposed to wind and water is slowly worn away or dissolved. This is called weathering. Tiny bits fall off, and most are washed or blown into rivers and carried to the sea where they pile up on the seabed. Rain with carbon dioxide dissolved in it is acidic. Acid rain falling on rock also dissolves it. The water with dissolved rock joins the sea, where some of the rock falls back out as tiny grains. Both types of weathering make sediment—fine particles lying on top of the solid rock of the land or seabed.

Making more rock

Over millions of years, sediment piles up, squashing and heating up the lower layers so much that the material at the bottom of the pile eventually becomes a new kind of rock, called sedimentary rock. Now, dead organisms and their waste add to the sediment, but in Earth's early days, sedimentary rock was made just of weathered and changed rock. An example is sandstone, a flaky kind of rock made from sand.

All change

When igneous or sedimentary rock is heated but does not melt, its structure can change, making a third type of rock, called metamorphic rock. This forms where rock is squashed from above and heated from below. Examples are marble and gneiss.

Slave craton
Wyoming craton
North Atlantic craton
Superior craton
North China craton
Tanzania craton
Madagascar craton
Pilbara craton
Kalahari craton
Brazilian craton
Yilgarn craton

Oldest surviving cratons

Weathering

Sediment

Sediment
Compaction
Cementation
Sedimentary rock

INCREASING PRESSURE

Pressure from surface rocks

Metamorphic rock

Heat from Magma

Sedimentary rock

41

MAGNETIC EARTH

Earth works like a gigantic magnet, with a magnetic field that stretches far into space. For this reason, an iron needle allowed to move freely will line up along the north-south axis of Earth. This is the basis of a magnetic compass, used to help find directions.

Making the world magnet

The hottest part of Earth is the inner core. This heats the liquid metal of the outer core, producing convection currents, just like those in the mantle. The hot metal rises through the outer core and colder, denser molten metal falls. The iron and nickel in the outer core conduct electricity; as they move, they make a magnetic field. It's rather like a giant bar magnet deep within Earth, but not quite lined up with the North and South Poles. The magnetic poles lie about 11 degrees from the geographic poles.

Homing pigeon

MAGNETIC NAVIGATORS

Humans are not the only animals to navigate using Earth's magnetic field. Some others, including migrating birds, probably detect it and use it to find their way on their long journeys.

Stretching into space

In space, the magnetic field forms Earth's protective magnetosphere. This diverts the charged particles of the solar wind around Earth so that they don't shower down onto the planet. Without the magnetosphere, our atmosphere and water could be ripped away by the solar wind. Earth's magnetic field has existed for at least 3.5 billion years, and perhaps as much as 4.2 billion years.

Light show

The solar wind and magnetic field together make brilliant light displays, called aurorae, near the North and South Poles. Charged particles from the Sun are caught and accelerated by the magnetosphere. When they collide with the atmosphere, they release bursts of energy as light. The aurorae are swirling patterns of green, pink, and violet. The north and south displays always match.

Flipping poles

The giant magnetic field switches direction every few hundred thousand years. This means that sometimes the magnetic north is at the geographic north and sometimes it's at the geographic south. It last switched about 780,000 years ago. We might be heading for another change, as the field is weakening in places.

Magnetic
north
pole

Geographic
north pole

Earth's
axis at
23° tilt

Equator

Geographic
south pole

Magnetic
south pole

43

HOT AND COLD

Earth is heated by the Sun, by energy from the pressure of matter squashed together in the middle of the Earth, and by the decay of radioactive materials. The Sun produced less energy in Earth's early days, but there was more energy from the other two sources.

TOO HOT?

Hot, but not hot enough

Early on, the Sun was dimmer, producing around only two thirds of the heat it now pours into space. If everything else had been the same, Earth should have been a giant frozen snowball. It has been a giant snowball at times, but it isn't usually, and it wasn't four billion years ago. Something else was keeping it warm.

TOO COLD?

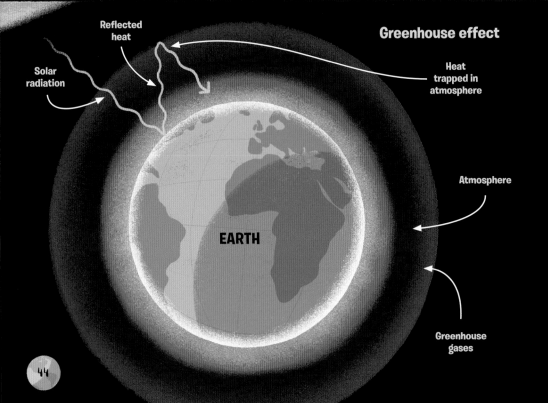

Greenhouse effect

Reflected heat

Solar radiation

Heat trapped in atmosphere

Atmosphere

EARTH

Greenhouse gases

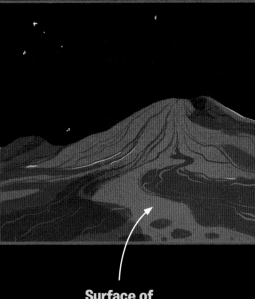

Surface of Venus

Unstable decay

Radioactive decay is the process of atoms of one element changing to atoms of another. It releases energy as heat, and this was one of Earth's early sources of heating.

Atoms contain a nucleus, usually composed of two types of particles, protons and neutrons. (Hydrogen alone has just a proton in the nucleus.) All atoms of an element have the same number of protons, but they can have different numbers of neutrons. Versions of an element with different numbers of neutrons are called isotopes. Some isotopes are unstable. Their atoms slowly decay, reducing the number of protons they have, and so changing them from one element to another. If the new atom is also unstable, it decays again. When an atom reaches a stable state, it won't decay any more. The heat from radioactive decay is steadily dropping as many of the atoms that were unstable have already decayed.

JUST RIGHT FOR LIVING THINGS

GREENHOUSE PLANET

The planet Venus has a thick atmosphere of carbon dioxide, producing an extreme greenhouse effect. Its surface temperature is 462°C (864°F). Mercury is colder, even though it's closer to the Sun. With no insulating atmosphere, it is 400°C (750°F) by day and −200°C (−330°F) at night.

A warm blanket

Long ago, Earth's atmosphere contained a lot of carbon dioxide and methane. Both of these are greenhouse gases—they trap heat near Earth rather then letting it escape into space. Heat from accretion, radioactive decay, and the Sun was trapped near the surface and built up, keeping Earth warm.

Hotter and colder periods in Earth's past have all been linked with how much greenhouse gas is in the atmosphere. A thicker layer of greenhouse gases makes Earth hotter. A thinner layer lets heat escape, and Earth cools. Now, human activities are making greenhouse gases build up, warming Earth.

LIFE STARTS

With a surface of rock and seawater beneath a protective, warming atmosphere, early Earth was ready to host its first life. Scientists are not quite sure when or how life first started. If life began before the Moon's violent formation, the event would have wiped it out and it would have had to start over again. The ancestors of current life might have appeared as early as 4.4 billion years ago, just after the formation of the Moon, or perhaps a few hundred million years later. They were simple micro-organisms with just a single cell, but even those changed Earth beyond recognition.

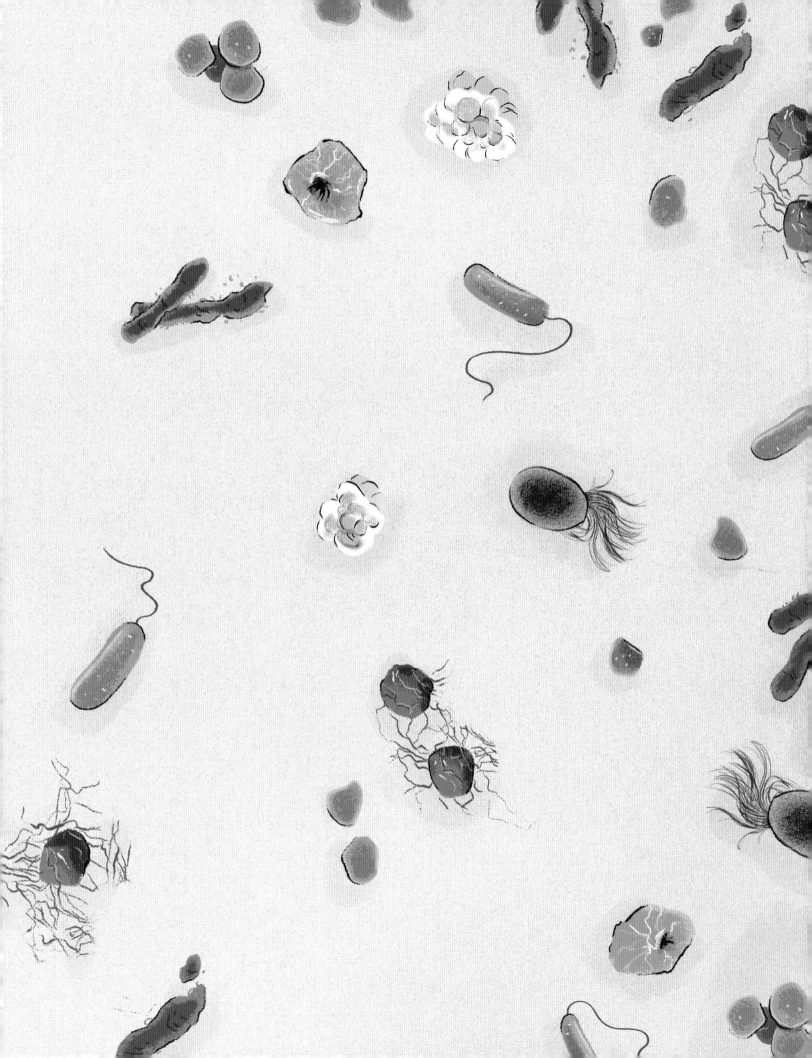

STEPPING TOWARD LIFE

For life to have emerged, chemicals must have copied themselves and separated from their environment in some kind of package or capsule. And these two steps must have come together in conditions that existed on early Earth.

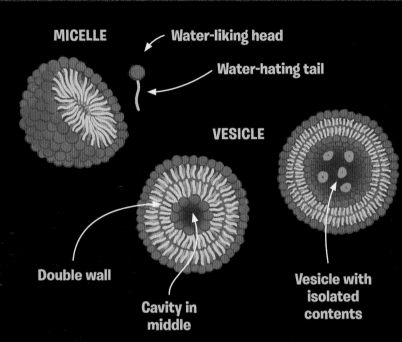

MICELLE

Water-liking head

Water-hating tail

VESICLE

Double wall

Cavity in middle

Vesicle with isolated contents

Cut off from the world

Chemicals can just make copies of themselves without needing to be contained, but living things have an outside that separates them from the rest of the world. This can form from simple chemicals, too.

Molecules of some chemicals naturally cluster to make little balls or pouches. They have one end that is attracted to water and one end that is repelled by water. They group with the water-hating ends jammed together in the middle. These clusters are called **micelles**.

If they grow large or join together, they can make a double-walled pocket that has the water-hating ends hidden inside the wall and water-liking ends in the water outside, and surrounding a drop of water in the middle. These are **vesicles**. They grow larger by poaching molecules from other nearby micelles or vesicles. When they become too large, smaller ones easily break off if they are disturbed, such as by moving water.

If the water inside the vesicle contained self-replicating chemicals, the result could be self-replicating pockets, with the insides eventually becoming chemically quite different from the outside environment. This could be a step toward the first living things.

Asteroid

Copying chemicals

The chemical at the heart of most living things is DNA. It's a large molecule shaped like a twisted ladder (called a double helix). It can split in two along its length. Each half then rebuilds the other half to complete itself again. A slightly simpler chemical, called RNA, can also build copies of itself. All RNA and DNA need to make more of themselves is a supply of the necessary chemicals and the right conditions. Scientists think that some chemical, probably simpler than RNA, set the ball rolling by copying itself—self-replicating—in Earth's early oceans or pools. Lightning or even radiation from the Sun might have provided the energy to kick-start the process.

IT CAME FROM OUTER SPACE

Some scientists think that the first life forms, or the chemicals that could give rise to life, came from space, delivered on the asteroids that collided with Earth. This idea is called "panspermia." It doesn't really explain how life starts, though—it just shifts the problem elsewhere.

DNA

RNA

Double helix

An RNA molecule looks a bit like a DNA molecule split in half vertically.

ALIVE!

It's hard to decide exactly what life is. We can all say confidently that a rock is not alive, but a seagull or an oak tree is—but how do we draw the line? How do we define life? A simple definition says living things must be able to reproduce (make more of themselves) and grow, and they need a source of energy. Scientists often consider that a living thing must have at least one cell, and complex organisms like humans and trees have trillions of cells.

Small and simple

The smallest and simplest thing that might be considered living is a virus, but viruses don't have even one cell. They are on the border between living and non-living things, and so perhaps they show us how life might have stepped over that line. The simplest viruses are just a string of genetic material—a chemical code that acts like a "recipe" for making the virus—wrapped in an envelope of protein. They can reproduce only inside a living cell in another, "host," organism, though they can survive for a while outside a cell. They don't have a way of capturing and using energy and they don't grow, feed, breathe, or move around on their own. All they can do is reproduce. To do that, they hijack parts of the cell they infect, using its resources to make more virus particles. If viruses count as living, they are the most numerous living things on the planet.

Sponge

FUNGI

PLANTS

Amoeba

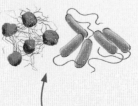

PROKARYOTES (NO NUCLEUS)
Archaea and bacteria

Lively cells

The smallest things that can definitely be called "alive" are microorganisms such as bacteria and archaea. These have a single, simple cell. They can reproduce, some can move on their own, and they take energy

Worm

Squid

Mosquito

DATING LIFE

A new way of working out how long ago differences between organisms might have appeared suggests that the earliest life formed soon after the impact that created the Moon. Both bacteria and archaea developed from these first life-forms.

Parrotfish

Blue tit

Blue whale

INVERTEBRATES

ANIMALS

MULTI-CELLULAR ORGANISMS

EUKARYOTES (WITH NUCLEUS)

VERTEBRATES

Fox

and chemicals from their surroundings to build their bodies and function. There are lots of sources of energy available to organisms. You take your energy from food, as do all other animals. Plants take their energy from sunlight. Bacteria and archaea first took their energy from chemicals in water or rock, and sometimes from heat or light. The processes the earliest cells used to gain energy still happen, but now often as part of something far more complex.

NOT A NICE LIVING SPACE

The first living things probably emerged in the sea, or in pools of water on the patches of rocky land, and perhaps even in or under ice.

Extremophiles, then and now

Early Earth was a hostile place. Wherever organisms first appeared, they would have had to deal with extreme conditions. Shallow surface pools would have been blasted by harmful radiation from the Sun. Some places could have been very hot and others very cold. Organisms that live in such conditions now are called extremophiles. They can survive in scalding, acidic water, beneath the ice sheets, and even deep within rocks. Early life could have colonized any of these places.

Hydrothermal pools

The bright green, blue, orange and yellow of the volcanic pools in Yellowstone National Park, USA, are produced by heat-loving extremophile bacteria that live in the water.

The water isn't lovely

The first life probably emerged in water, and survived only in wet environments. But water on early Earth was not always inviting. Good places for organisms that needed chemicals or heat as their source of energy would have been volcanically active, with warm or hot water rich in chemicals.

Deep under the sea, hydrothermal vents are still home to extremophiles. These undersea chimneys pour out scalding water heated in the mantle. The water is rich in chemicals that microorganisms might use as a source of energy, but it's acidic and very hot. The area around them is completely dark, being in the deep sea.

On land, hot water bubbles rise to the surface in hydrothermal pools in volcanically active areas.

Hydrothermal vents

Hydrothermal vents still support extremophiles. Microorganisms use the chemicals such as iron, sulfur compounds, and ammonia in the hot water. Larger organisms, such as strange tube worms, snails, and crabs, feed on them and each other, making an entire extremophile ecosystem.

Tube worms

Antarctic ice sheet

Subglacial lake

Bacteria are found living in lakes hidden deep under the ice of Antarctica, and even in rock that is apparently solid, but has tiny spaces inside. In one lake, under 800 m (2,625 ft) of solid ice, nearly 4,000 types of archae and bacteria live. They have evolved in isolation for at least 120,000 years and perhaps a million years.

CYCLING AND RECYCLING

Earth is the ultimate recycler. A little matter arrives from space or is lost to space, but almost everything on Earth is constantly recycled. You drink the same water dinosaurs drank, and the carbon in your body has been in the atmosphere, in rocks, and in other organisms.

Water stored as snow and ice

Precipitation (snow)

Melted snow runs in streams

Water evaporates from ground and plants

Precipitation (rain)

Water runs over the ground

Evaporation

Water stored in lakes and pools

Water runs through the ground

Water stored in the ground

Reusable atoms

Atoms are infinitely reusable. They can combine to make different compounds, which can then break down, freeing the atoms to be used again. The same atoms have been on Earth since the planet formed, and even after Earth ends they will be reused in something else, perhaps in another planet or moon, or perhaps in more living things of some type.

Water stored in clouds

Condensation

Water evaporates from the sea

Water stored in oceans

Recycling, fast and slow

The solid rock of Earth's surface began to be recycled as soon as it formed. Acid rain and weathering break down rock, freeing chemicals that are then washed into the sea or which escape into the atmosphere. They are eventually made into new rock. It's a slow process. A single carbon atom takes 100–200 million years to complete the cycle from rock, through ocean and atmosphere, back to rock.

Life added much quicker cycles. Once there were living things, there were soon dead things. When organisms died, their tiny, single cells drifted to the seabed or lakebed and added to the sediment there. At some point, bacteria evolved that could break down the dead cells and recycle the chemicals in them. Chemicals from some organisms eventually became new rock, made from the sediment.

No wasted water

It's not only elements like carbon, nitrogen and oxygen that move through cycles. All the water on Earth is recycled, too. The water cycle is important to life. It is affected by the temperature, as water can exist as a solid, liquid, or gas on Earth. When the global temperature is low, a lot of water is locked away in ice. When it's hotter, less water is stored in ice and the sea levels are higher.

Water evaporates from the ocean, the ground, rivers, and lakes, then condenses as clouds and falls as rain. Rain that falls on the land can either run through the ground or be carried back to the sea by rivers to start the cycle again.

LIFE IN THE LIGHT

Sunlight powers life on Earth today. Plants and algae use energy from the Sun to make new chemicals with those they take from water and the air. This process, called photosynthesis, provides the food and oxygen on which all life depends. From the smallest plant to a mighty cloud leopard, all lifeforms ultimately get their energy from sunlight.

Starting with heat

Early life clustered in the sea. There was little land, and it was blasted by high levels of radiation. The sea was a safe haven. In the depths, no light penetrated and microorganisms lived out their lives in darkness, metabolizing chemicals in seawater. But sunlight filtered through shallow water, at the coast and in pools and rivers. Around 3.4 billion years ago, some microbes began to use the heat of sunlight as a source of energy.

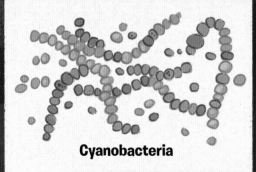

Cyanobacteria

Making light work

Then about 2.7 billion years ago, a different type of photosynthesizing organism evolved, called cyanobacteria. Instead of using heat (infrared radiation), cyanobacteria used visible light from the Sun and released oxygen. This was one of the most important steps in the evolution of life on Earth. Now, all green plants photosynthesize in this way, using energy from sunlight to produce the chemicals they need to live and grow, and releasing oxygen.

EATEN ALIVE!

The parts of a plant cell that carry out photosynthesis are called chloroplasts. Billions of years ago, chloroplasts were independent microorganisms. They were absorbed by other cells and carried on working inside them.

A fair swap

A photosynthesizing plant uses the energy of sunlight to make a sugar— called glucose—from water and carbon dioxide. Oxygen is a waste product, and is released into the air or water. For every molecule of glucose a plant makes, it releases 12 atoms of oxygen. That oxygen is used by almost all other living things, which need oxygen to survive. Plants use the glucose they make as a source of energy and as a step in making the chemicals they need to build a stem, leaves, roots, flowers, and seeds. Animals gain their energy from eating plants or other animals. Without photosynthesizing plants and microbes, life on Earth as we know it couldn't exist.

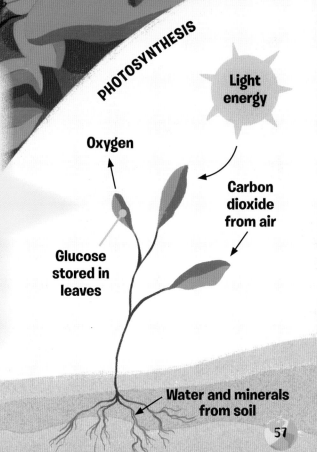

PHOTOSYNTHESIS

Light energy

Oxygen

Carbon dioxide from air

Glucose stored in leaves

Water and minerals from soil

OXYGEN OVERLOAD

Cyanobacteria that used carbon dioxide and produced oxygen were very successful. They were using a resource—visible light in sunlight—that was not useful to other organisms, so there was no competition and they flourished in shallow seas.

Come to the light

Cyanobacteria lived near the surface of the water and at the coasts, where water is shallow enough for light to get through. This forced other organisms into the deeper sea where cyanobacteria could not survive. It made little difference to the other organisms, so did no harm at first.

Cyanobacteria lived on top of the bodies of their ancestors that piled up and hardened into rock beneath them over millions of years. These rocky mounds are called stromatolites. As cyanobacteria could get the most sunlight by being closest to the surface of the water, those on top of the mounds were more successful, so kept going, with the mounds building up. Cyanobacteria still make stromatolites.

Stromatolite

Fresh air

At first, the oxygen released by photosynthesizing cyanobacteria dissolved in the seawater around them. They were so successful that eventually they produced too much oxygen for it to stay dissolved. The sea contained dissolved iron, and the oxygen reacted with this to make iron oxide, or rust. Rust doesn't dissolve in water and it fell to the sea bed. There it was trapped in the forming sedimentary rock. Soon, there was even too much oxygen for that, and the sea ran out of dissolved iron. Oxygen began to escape into the atmosphere, adding the first, small, portion of the gas we now all need to breathe.

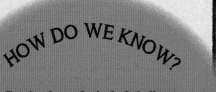

HOW DO WE KNOW?

Rocks from 2.4–2.0 billion years ago show broad stripes of red, made of rust deposited on the seabed and trapped in forming rock. Iron-banded rocks are found around the world. Much of the iron we now mine was laid down at this time.

Rust stripes in rock

Blooming algae

At the same time as cyanobacteria were pouring out oxygen, rock was weathering and sediment was washing into the sea. The extra nutrients the water carried supported even more cyanobacteria, resulting in yet more oxygen. Sediment piled up on the seabed, covering some of the substances that could have reacted with some of the oxygen, so even more escaped into the atmosphere. The change to the atmosphere is called the Great Oxygenation Event; it lasted from around 2.4 billion years ago to around 2.1 billion years ago.

CATASTROPHIC COLD

The effect of vast blooms of cyanobacteria was catastrophic. They poured oxygen first into the ocean and then into the atmosphere, changing Earth forever. Cyanobacteria caused the Earth's first mass extinction event—a mass dying of microorganisms.

Out of the greenhouse, into the freezer

Oxygen was poisonous to many of the other microbes that lived in the water, and it began to kill them. But far worse was to come. Oxygen in the atmosphere reacted with methane, producing carbon dioxide and water. Methane is a very potent greenhouse gas, and kept enough heat close to Earth to keep the planet warm. Carbon dioxide has only about one twentieth the greenhouse effect of methane, so Earth began to cool. At the same time, by flooding the shallows with oxygen, cyanobacteria drove the methane-producing microbes into the deeper sea. They could live there, but the methane they made could not escape into the atmosphere.

As if that wasn't enough, rock was breaking apart and weathering. The weathering process used up some of the new carbon dioxide, reducing greenhouse gases even more. With less greenhouse gas, Earth's heat could escape more easily into space. The planet cooled so much that from a balmy, wet paradise for microbes it turned into a hostile, icy wasteland.

Snowball Earth

Nearly 2.3 billion years ago, most or all of Earth's surface was frozen, covered by an ice sheet that stretched from pole to pole. It stayed frozen for around 100 million years. That's the equivalent of Earth freezing when the dinosaurs died and still being frozen today—and staying frozen for the next 35 million years. What looked at first like just a small change—microorganisms using light instead of heat—turned into a total catastrophe. The temperature plunged as low as -50°C in some times and places.

Ice or slush?

We don't know exactly what Earth was like during this first "Snowball Earth" event. The entire planet might have been covered in a thick, unbroken ice sheet. Or there might have been pockets of unfrozen surface water, creating a more slushy snowball in some areas.

ALIVE UNDER THE ICE

Somehow, life kept going under the ice sheet. If pockets of water remained unfrozen, life—including the oxygen-producing culprits—could cling on for the millions of years it took for the global snowball to warm and eventually melt.

ACTIVE EARTH

When the ice of Snowball Earth finally began to melt, it was because of the planet's own activity. Earth's geological activity did not stop or slow down when the surface froze. There is always a lot going on deep inside, and over millions of years this finally freed the frozen planet from its icy shroud.

Geologists recognize three states of Earth—snowball, icehouse, and greenhouse. Snowball Earth is covered or nearly covered with ice, with frozen land and sea extending far from the poles. Icehouse Earth has some surface ice, as now. Greenhouse Earth is warm, with no permanent ice, even at the poles.

MELTING THE SNOWBALL

For the ice to melt, Earth needed to warm up. Earth's heat was escaping into space because the protective blanket of greenhouse gases had been eaten away by the addition of oxygen to the atmosphere. It could only be fixed by adding more greenhouse gases. Luckily, that's exactly what happened.

Reknitting the blanket

When rocks were covered with ice, there was no weathering, so carbon dioxide wasn't removed from the atmosphere. But Earth's volcanoes still poured out carbon dioxide and vaporized water. More carbon dioxide built up over millions of years, creating a new blanket of greenhouse gas. Eventually, it warmed the planet enough to melt the ice.

The inorganic carbon cycle regulates Earth's climate over millions of years. It is too slow to help us reverse the global heating caused by the extra carbon dioxide we are pouring into the atmosphere now.

Carbon cycles

In warm times, carbon dioxide from the atmosphere dissolves in rain water, making it slightly acidic. This slowly corrodes the rock it falls on. The run-off water carries minerals from the rock into rivers and eventually to the sea. Minerals are deposited on the seabed, including carbon as carbonates, making new rock. At the edges of the ocean, the seabed is slowly pulled back into Earth's mantle and melts. Carbon dioxide freed from carbonate rocks rises up through volcanoes and back into the atmosphere in eruptions. Some of it dissolves in rain and begins the cycle again. This cycling of carbon through rocks, ocean, and atmosphere is called the inorganic carbon cycle. (It's "inorganic" because it doesn't involve organic life—organisms.)

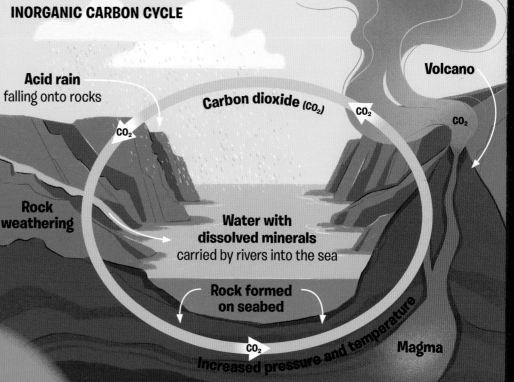

INORGANIC CARBON CYCLE

Volcano

Acid rain falling onto rocks

CO_2

Carbon dioxide (CO_2)

CO_2

CO_2

Rock weathering

Water with dissolved minerals carried by rivers into the sea

Rock formed on seabed

CO_2

Increased pressure and temperature

Magma

HOT AND COLD, COLD AND HOT

Earth has had several snowball events. When the ice melts, rocks are again exposed and begin to weather, taking carbon dioxide out of the atmosphere. If too much carbon dioxide is removed too quickly, Earth freezes again and has to wait for carbon dioxide to build up once more. Snowball events tend be broken up by brief warm periods for this reason.

Now, calcium carbonate from the sea is used by sea animals to build their shells.

BROKEN PLATES

Earth's crust of hard rock floats on top of the thick, gooey, semi-molten rock of the mantle. As the magma moves below it, the crust is dragged slowly around the globe. Our planet is always shifting and changing beneath our feet, though usually too slowly for us to notice.

A rocky puzzle

Earth's crust is broken into chunks, called tectonic plates. They fit together perfectly, like the pieces of a jigsaw puzzle. Some plates carry continental land, with its mountains, plains, rivers, and lakes. Others carry ocean—a thin layer of rock flooded with water. The continental plates have built up around cratons that are very old, and some of the rock of the continental plates is billions of years old. The ocean plates are made of newer but heavier rock.

This rock is constantly renewed and the oldest is only about 145 million years old.

There are seven major plates and a number of smaller plates. The largest is the Pacific plate, which holds the whole of the Pacific Ocean. It covers an area of 103 million square km (40 million square mi)—more than a quarter of Earth's surface. Although the rock of the seabed is not very old, the plate as a piece of the jigsaw is probably at least three billion years old.

Jiggling jigsaw

All the tectonic plates move with the magma beneath them, but they don't all move in the same direction. The magma moves in convection cells as rock heats up, rises, cools and falls again. As a result, sometimes plates move apart, sometimes they collide, and sometimes they grate against each other. All these types of movement have dramatic effects at Earth's surface, including explosive volcanic eruptions, devastating earthquakes and growing mountains.

Active edges

There are three types of boundaries between plates. They describe how the plates on each side of the boundary are moving.

TECTONIC PLATES TODAY

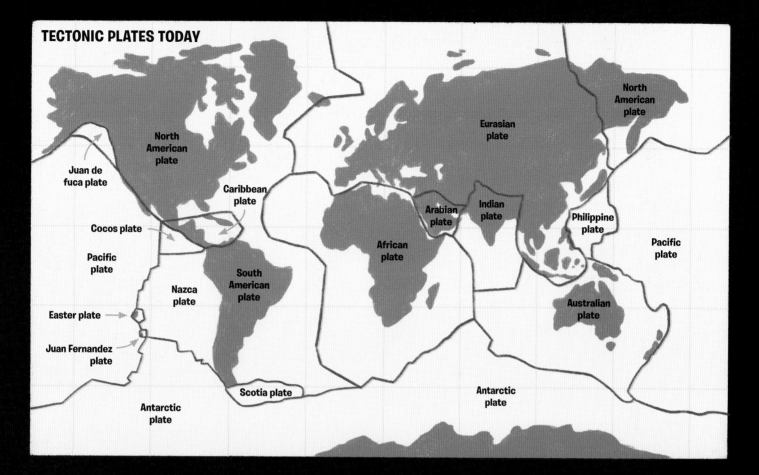

North American plate

Juan de fuca plate

Caribbean plate

Cocos plate

Pacific plate

Nazca plate

Easter plate

Juan Fernandez plate

South American plate

Antarctic plate

Scotia plate

Eurasian plate

Arabian plate

Indian plate

African plate

Philippine plate

Pacific plate

Australian plate

North American plate

Antarctic plate

At a **constructive boundary**, plates pull apart and magma wells up through the gap, hardening into new rock. This happens in the middle of the oceans and where continental plates are rifting (coming apart).

At a **destructive boundary**, plates crash together. As they crunch into each other, one can be forced under the other. If rock piles up at the join, mountains form.

At a **conservative boundary**, the plates move alongside each other. No new rock is created, but the edges grate against each other.

Continental crust

Mantle rocks

Oceanic crust

Where ocean meets land, a destructive boundary often forms, the plates moving toward each other.

67

NEW ROCK FOR OLD

New rock forms where tectonic plates move apart and magma oozes out from below. It's part of a long, slow process of recycling rock through Earth's crust and mantle.

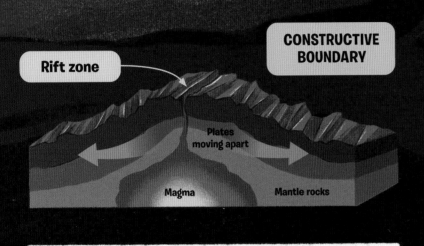

CONSTRUCTIVE BOUNDARY

Rift zone

Plates moving apart

Magma

Mantle rocks

Splitting apart

Where tectonic plates are moving apart, a rift zone forms. A rift stretches all the way through the Atlantic Ocean, from the sea east of Greenland in the north, to the bottom of South America. Most of this rift is under the sea, but it also passes straight through Iceland, an island between Greenland and the northern European countries of Scandinavia. Iceland is very volcanically active. Volcanoes pour out lava and gases regularly, and sometimes new islands appear off the coast, made by magma erupting and hardening under the sea.

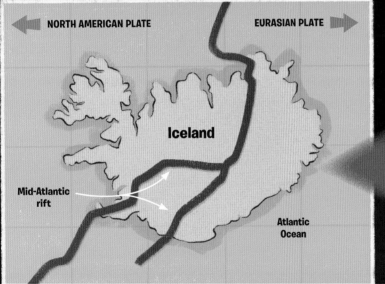

NORTH AMERICAN PLATE

EURASIAN PLATE

Iceland

Mid-Atlantic rift

Atlantic Ocean

Two other overland rift zones are in Africa, where moving plates are pulling the continent apart. Eventually sea will flood the area and the east part of Africa will separate from most of the continent—but this will happen millions of years in the future.

Mountains and valleys

The magma that leaks from a mid-ocean rift piles up and hardens on either side of the rift. As the plates pull apart, the piled-up rock moves slowly away from the rift on both sides, making a range of mountains either side of a dip (the active rift). These are not small cracks—the rift in the middle of the Atlantic Ocean is about the size of the Grand Canyon in North America. In the Pacific Ocean, where the plates move faster, the rock doesn't stay still long enough to make vast mountains, and forms a plain instead. The ocean bed has a dramatic landscape of mountains, valleys and plains hidden beneath the waves.

The mid-Atlantic rift joins up with rifts that run below Africa and Australia and also meets the mid-Pacific rift zone, making the largest mountain range on Earth, at 65,000 km (40,000 mi) long.

Europe

Africa

MID-ATLANTIC RIFT

South
America

Underwater
mountain range

GROWING OCEANS

As the seabed either side of the Atlantic rift zone pulls in opposite directions, the Americas on one side and Europe and Africa on the other side move further apart. The Atlantic Ocean grows wider by about 2–5 cm (0.8– 2 in) every year, or 2 m (6.5 ft) every century. Parts of the Pacific grow 6–16 cm (3–6 in) a year.

ROCK MEETS WATER

While the plates at a rift zone pull apart, the opposite ends of those plates are also moving and need to go somewhere. The edges of the oceanic plates meet the continental coasts. The rock doesn't just pile up there—instead, it is pulled back into the mantle and recycled.

Subduction zones

At the coast, an oceanic plate collides with a continental plate. The two plates are moving toward each other, and one has to give way. The oceanic plate is densest, and dips below the lighter continental plate. It's pulled deep into the mantle and melts. The place where this happens is called a subduction zone. The rock that melts here formed at the mid-ocean rift up to 150 million years before.

The water in the seabed lowers the melting point of the magma, and the magma along the edge of the continental plate melts. It rises through the crust, forming volcanoes. Most of Earth's volcanoes are along subduction zones. Lava from the volcanoes sticks to the edge of the continental plate, slowly making it larger.

The slab of seabed spends millions of years on its journey toward the bottom of the mantle. The pull on it going down into the mantle and the push of the new rock growing at the mid-ocean rift work together to move the seabed toward the continental coast.

Mid-ocean rift

Oceanic trench

Oceanic crust

Hydrothermal vent

Magma

SEA IS NOT OCEAN

The world's oceans are all connected and all are on oceanic crust. Earth also has seas, some of which are inland and are flooded areas of continental crust. The Mediterranean Sea, in Europe, is a stranded portion of oceanic crust. As it's not subducted and recycled, it's much older than the crust below the oceans, at up to 340 million years old.

Deep and dark

Deep trenches form at a subduction zone where the oceanic plate is pulled down. These are quite close to the coast, but have the deepest seas on Earth. The very deepest is the Mariana Trench in the western Pacific Ocean, between Japan and Papua New Guinea. It is nearly 11 km (6.8 mi) at its deepest, and is 2550 km (1,580 mi) long and 69 km (43 mi) wide.

Volcano

Continental crust

Magma

Oceanic crust

Subducting plate

SUBDUCTION ZONE

Magma

MOUNTAIN-BUILDING

Not all collisions are between one plate carrying land and one plate carrying ocean. Sometimes, two continental plates collide. Neither is lighter than the other, and it's not clear which should give way.

Tall and deep

The pile of rock that makes a mountain is very heavy, so it sinks some way into the mantle below. The more rock that piles up, the heavier the mountains become and the lower they lie. The result is that mountains have deep "roots"—blobs of rock far underground that burrow into the mantle. Mountains grow both upward and downward.

The tallest mountains in the world, the Himalayas, formed as the continental plate carrying India pushed into the Eurasian plate that carries Europe and most of Asia. Eighty million years ago, India was an island lying 6,400 km (3,968 mi) south of the land that is now Tibet, but started moving northward.

Vanishing oceans, growing mountains

Sometimes continental plates move toward each other, squeezing out an area of ocean between them until it closes up. Then continental plates collide. After the oceanic crust has all been subducted, the continental plates push relentlessly together. The rock rucks and folds, rising in the middle and piling up, first into hills, and eventually into mountains.

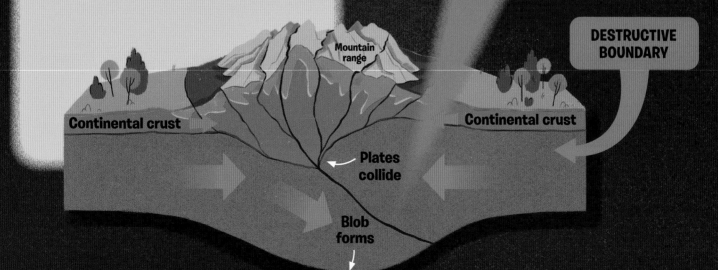

Mountain range

Continental crust

Continental crust

DESTRUCTIVE BOUNDARY

Plates collide

Blob forms

AS OLD AS THE HILLS

The world's oldest mountains are the Appalachians. These started to grow around 480 million years ago, forced up by plates colliding as they combined to make a new continent. The mountains continued to grow and change for hundreds of millions of years, but are now eroding. Mountains in Sweden, Greenland, and Scotland are all part of the same mountain range as the Appalachians, torn apart by the shifting continents.

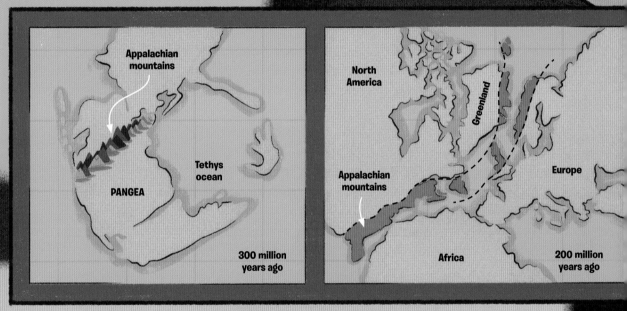

Appalachian mountains

Tethys ocean

PANGEA

300 million years ago

North America

Greenland

Appalachian mountains

Africa

Europe

200 million years ago

Swapping sea for mountains

India crashed into Eurasia 50 million years ago and is still forcing its way north. The Tethys ocean that lay between the two plates has now gone. The pressure has pushed up the Himalayas, which grow taller at a rate of 2 cm (0.8 in) a year and are still sinking deeper into the mantle. As well as piling up mountains, the pressure pushes up the land behind the mountains, making a high, flat plateau. The plateau of Tibet has no mountains itself, but is higher than the mountaintops of the Alps in Europe.

Rock folding

GRINDING AND CRUNCHING

Land isn't created or destroyed at every plate boundary. At conservative boundaries, tectonic plates grate alongside each other in different directions or at different speeds. Much of the time, everything is calm—but not always.

Tense moments

Tectonic plates don't have smooth edges that glide past one another easily. They are jagged and heavy, and spend much of their time snagged against each other. The slow flow of magma below pushes them onward, so pressure builds up. When that pressure gets to be too much, the plates free themselves and suddenly jerk forward. The result at the surface is an earthquake—the ground shakes and even breaks apart, the shock reverberating through the planet. An earthquake under the sea can produce a tsunami—a massive wave that floods over the land, often with devastating results.

Plate

Plate

CONSERVATIVE
BOUNDARY

Earth's faults

One of the most active earthquake zones is the San Andreas fault in the USA. It runs 1,300 km (800 mi) through most of California, joining another fault line that runs for a further 1,300 km into Mexico. Other danger areas include the coast of South America and northern border of India. The largest fault line is the Sunda Megathrust in Southeast Asia, which is 5,500 km long (3400 mi) and runs from Myanmar to Australia. An earthquake here in 2004 caused a tsunami that killed 230,000 people.

Waves, in and out of the sea

A tsunami, like an ordinary wave, is energy moving through water rather than water itself moving far. An earthquake produces huge waves of energy, called seismic waves, which ripple through Earth—not just through the land and sea, but also the mantle and even the core.

Tsunami

Shaken apart

Seismic waves can tear apart roads, bridges, and brick or concrete buildings. These can't ripple or bend to absorb the shock and they crumble under the stress of an earthquake. Earthquakes are less dangerous in the countryside, or where buildings are made of flexible materials. Most people who are hurt are harmed by falling buildings, or a tsunami flooding the land.

SEEING INSIDE

Waves of energy travel at different speeds through different materials. By tracking the movement and speed of seismic waves, geologists have worked out the internal structure of Earth, finding the boundaries between the mantle, outer core, and inner core.

INSIDE A VOLCANO

Volcanoes cluster along plate boundaries. They form where magma wells up from the mantle to the crust. Some are mountains, but others are more like cracks in the ground or seabed. When a volcano erupts, it can hurl out magma as lava in a devastating explosion—or just leak it gently.

A gallery of volcanoes

Inside a volcano, magma rises from a reservoir through tubes and channels that it melts in the rock. There are different types of volcano.

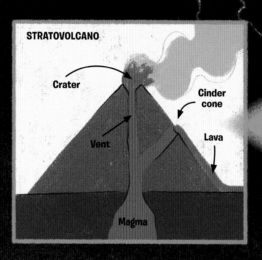

STRATOVOLCANO

Crater

Cinder cone

Vent

Lava

Magma

Stratovolcanoes are fed by slabs of sinking seabed melting at the edge of the ocean. Magma collects beneath the volcano, melting the rock around it. When the pressure of molten rock becomes too great, the volcanic mountain can blow apart. These are the most violent eruptions, spewing runny, scalding lava into the air and over the land. Stratovolcanoes often have smaller cinder cone volcanoes on their slopes.

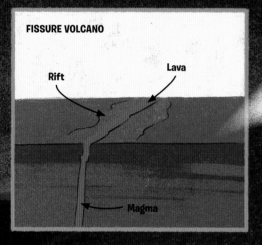

FISSURE VOLCANO

Rift

Lava

Magma

Fissure volcanoes are rifts in the ground where plates are pulling apart. They don't have sudden, violent eruptions but steadily ooze lava.

Hotspot volcanoes are the only type that can occur in the middle of a tectonic plate rather than just at the edges. They are huge **shield volcanoes** with shallow slopes and grow over a "hotspot" where magma rises from deep in the mantle. As Earth's crust slowly moves over the hotspot, a chain of volcanoes forms. The Hawaiian Islands are volcanoes formed over a hotspot below the Pacific Ocean.

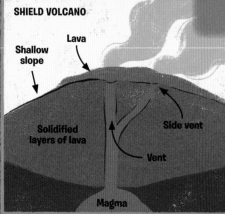

SHIELD VOLCANO

Lava

Shallow slope

Solidified layers of lava

Side vent

Vent

Magma

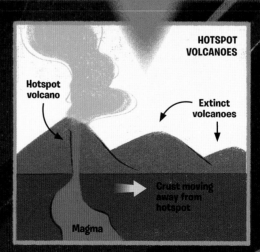

HOTSPOT VOLCANOES

Hotspot volcano

Extinct volcanoes

Crust moving away from hotspot

Magma

Biggest and best (or worst)

The largest volcanoes are **supervolcanoes**. They erupt with such violence that they can lay waste to vast areas. There have been only 42 eruptions of this type in the last 36 million years. The most famous supervolcano is in Yellowstone Park, USA. It is fed from a hotspot below that has been active for at least 16 million years. It last erupted about 630,000 years ago.

SUPERVOLCANO

PREHISTORIC SUPERVOLCANO

The supervolcano Toba in Indonesia erupted 75,000 years ago, long before human civilization began. The largest eruption of the last two million years, It hurled matter at least 10 km (6.2 mi) into the air, and ash covered an area half the size of the USA.

MAKING AND BREAKING CONTINENTS

As the crust crawls around the globe over millions of years, continental plates combine and break apart, and oceans open and close. The size and position of continents are constantly changing.

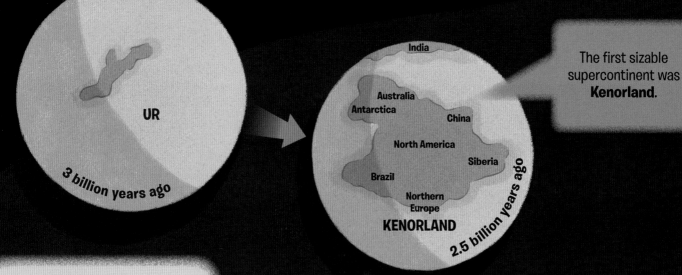

UR

3 billion years ago

The first sizable supercontinent was **Kenorland**.

India
Australia
Antarctica
China
North America
Siberia
Brazil
Northern Europe
KENORLAND

2.5 billion years ago

Continents and supercontinents

People noticed long ago that the bulge of the west coast of Africa fits neatly into the curve of the east coast of Central and Southern America. Millions of years ago, these lands were joined together—as was most of the land on Earth. It formed a single, large supercontinent now called Pangea, which began to break up 200 million years ago. Pangea was just the last in a sequence of supercontinents. A supercontinent has all or most of Earth's land grouped together. Supercontinents come and go, as the movement of the plates brings them together and splits them apart.

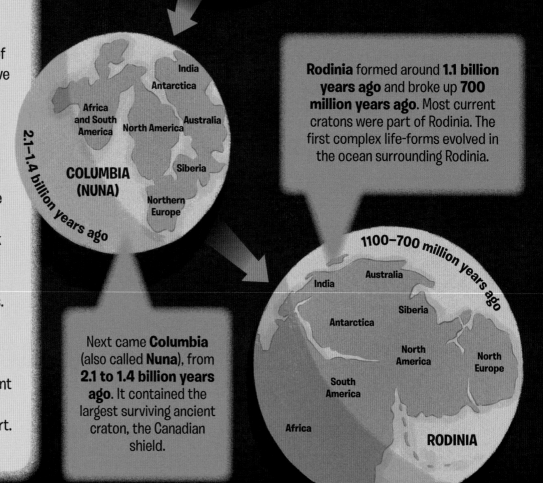

India
Antarctica
Africa and South America
North America
Australia
Siberia
COLUMBIA (NUNA)
Northern Europe

2.1–1.4 billion years ago

Rodinia formed around **1.1 billion years ago** and broke up **700 million years ago**. Most current cratons were part of Rodinia. The first complex life-forms evolved in the ocean surrounding Rodinia.

Next came **Columbia** (also called **Nuna**), from **2.1 to 1.4 billion years ago**. It contained the largest surviving ancient craton, the Canadian shield.

1100–700 million years ago

India
Australia
Antarctica
Siberia
North America
North Europe
South America
Africa
RODINIA

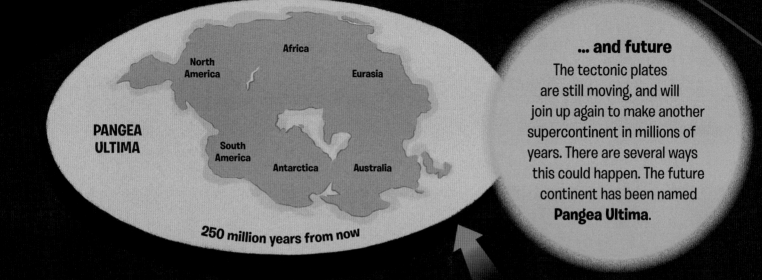

PANGEA ULTIMA

Africa
North America
Eurasia
South America
Antarctica
Australia

250 million years from now

... and future
The tectonic plates are still moving, and will join up again to make another supercontinent in millions of years. There are several ways this could happen. The future continent has been named **Pangea Ultima**.

Supercontinents of the past ...
Geologists don't agree about the first supercontinent. There is little evidence to work from. It might have been a tiny block of two cratons that are now small parts of South Africa and Australia, that combined 3.6 billion years ago to make "Vaalbara." There's more agreement about Ur, which is now part of Australia, Africa (Madagascar), and India. Although it was smaller than Australia is now, It counts as a supercontinent because it held most of the land; much of Earth was covered by ocean.

CONTINENTS TODAY

North America
Europe
Asia
Africa
South America
Oceania
Antarctica

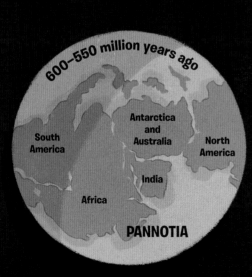

600–550 million years ago

South America
Antarctica and Australia
North America
India
Africa

PANNOTIA

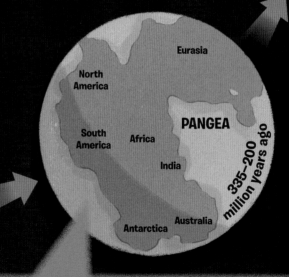

Eurasia
North America
South America
Africa
PANGEA
India
Antarctica
Australia

335–200 million years ago

The final supercontinent, **Pangea**, included 90 percent of Earth's land. It broke first into two large continents, Laurasia in the north and Gondwanaland in the south. These then split further and the parts slowly moved to their present positions.

LIVING PLANET

Charniodiscus

Rangea

Dickinsonia

Inaria

As snowball Earth melted 2.1 billion years ago, single-celled organisms herded into the unfrozen spaces. Over the next billion years, life was transformed, as cells came together to make the first multi-celled organisms. Within these organisms, cells specialized to take on different tasks, such as moving, gaining energy, or reproducing. Some organisms began to reproduce sexually, putting together genetic information from two parents instead of copying just one parent.

More snowball Earth events came and went until about 650 million years ago. The final thaw seems to have triggered an explosion of new life. The Ediacaran sea filled with strange, quilted, puffy organisms that looked like nothing alive today and had no obvious heads, mouths, or digestive organs.

Charnia

Haootia

Tribrachidium

Ernietta

Parvancorina

LIFE EXPLODES

Once life really got going, it burst into action. Around 540 million years ago, organisms grew larger, began to move more, and developed senses that helped them to compete with each other for living space and food.

An early arms race

Ediacaran organisms were either rooted to the seabed or moved slowly over it, grazing on the microbial mat. But in the Cambrian period, starting 542 million years ago, animals began to eat each other. In a rapid "arms race," some animals developed ways of catching and killing other animals. Their prey evolved to avoid being eaten. Weapons such as claws and teeth appeared. Prey animals developed hard outsides and shells to protect them from hungry mouths.

Opabinia

Marella

Seeing you, seeing me

Eyes evolved, so animals could see each other and their surroundings. Even single-celled organisms often have "eye spots"—patches that are sensitive to light and tell the organism where light is coming from. These can help an organism line itself up to take energy from sunlight or hide in the shadows. But true vision was a leap forward. For a prey animal, being able to see and hide from something wanting to eat you is important. For a predator, being able to spot your meal is just as important.

Hallucigenia

Anomalocaris

Move along

Both predators and prey evolved new ways of moving, whether to hunt or to escape. Creatures began to crawl, walk, and swim in different ways. Those that could move faster were often more successful and survived to breed, driving evolution toward ever faster movement.

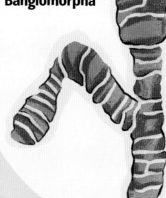

Bangiomorpha

The red alga *Bangiomorpha*, which lived a billion years ago, is the earliest known organism to reproduce sexually.

HOW DO WE KNOW?

The earliest large collections of fossils date from the Ediacaran and Cambrian periods, preserving the bodies of hundreds of thousands of early organisms. Some of them look very strange to our eyes, such as the five-eyed *Opabinia* with its clasper for grabbing prey, or the giant predator *Anomalocaris*.

Starting from here

Although few of the earliest animals look much like those we see now, many basic types of animals began half a billion years ago. The Ediacaran quilted organisms disappeared in a mass extinction, leaving only sponges, cnidarians (like jellyfish and corals) and simple worms to survive and evolve in the Cambrian period. All the main groups of animals alive now developed from these Cambrian organisms. Worms are still worms. Early arthropods have evolved into the insects, spiders, and crustaceans we have now. And the vertebrates that first appeared in the Cambrian period gave rise to fish, amphibians, reptiles, birds, and mammals.

Collinsium

Wiwaxia

83

ONTO THE LAND

Even during the Cambrian period, all life was still in the sea. The land was a harsh environment, with nothing but bare rock under a savage sun. Earth's surface was bombarded by damaging energy—the ultraviolet radiation in sunlight. This made the land too dangerous for anything except the hardiest microbes. But Earth's atmosphere was changing, and life on land soon became possible.

Burned by the light

The oxygen that cyanobacteria had begun to produce two billion years earlier changed the world again. About 500 million years ago, a layer of the gas ozone collected high in the atmosphere. Ozone is a form of oxygen, made of three oxygen atoms bound together. An ordinary oxygen molecule has two atoms bound together. Ultraviolet radiation splits apart some of the oxygen molecules in the atmosphere. Each of the two atoms then combines with another oxygen molecule to make ozone.

Free to roam

Ozone absorbs ultraviolet radiation, so a layer of ozone eventually made living on land safe. At least 420 million years ago (mya), the first land plants appeared. Unlike modern plants, they were simple stems that crept over the land, with no roots, leaves, or flowers. They reproduced from spores growing in fruiting bodies on the stems.

Animals followed the plants. Arthropods crept out of the water first, perhaps taking a short break where predators couldn't follow them, then adapting to full-time life on land. Next came "fishapods"— fish-like animals that hauled themselves over the mud on strong, prop-like fins that later evolved into legs.

Cooksonia
(433–393 mya)

Tiktaalik
(375 mya)

Getting dirty

The first soil was just tiny bits of rock and clay, mixed with microbes. Once plants and animals began to live on land, their waste made richer soils. Plants developed roots that held them securely in the soil and gave them a way of taking nutrients from it. Roots also held the soil in place so that it didn't easily blow or wash away. Slowly, the rocks gained a coating of soil and larger, more complex plants. Animals lived among the plants. Some of these animals ate the plants and others ate other animals. The land was at last alive.

FREAKY FUNGUS

Among the weird things that first grew on land was Prototaxites. Up to 8 m (26 ft) tall, it's thought to have been a giant fungus. Nothing like it and nothing descended from it is alive today.

Euryptids
(467–252 Ma)

Prototaxites
(470–360 mya)

REMAKING THE AIR

Changes to the atmosphere didn't end with the layer of ozone. The new life on land made possible by ozone had its own impact on the planet.

Life in the forest

As plants began to blanket the land, they led to another huge change in Earth's atmosphere. Vast forests grew, pouring more and more oxygen into the air.

Plants and animals first followed the path of rivers inland, but within 100 million years they had spread far and wide. Large areas were covered with lush forest. Earth's biomass (the mass of living things) increased to 800 times its previous level—the planet was truly teeming with life.

Meganeura

Arthropleura

Arthropods grew into giants—huge scorpions, millipedes up to 2 m (7 ft) long, and dragonflies the size of seagulls. Amphibians evolved from fishapods. They still laid their eggs in water, but lived largely on land as adults. From these, the reptiles evolved. Their eggs had a leathery shell that kept water inside, so they could be laid on land without drying out. That allowed the reptiles to move further away from the rivers and swamps. They could live deep in the forest and later even in parched areas like deserts. While amphibian eggs hatched into young quite different from their parents (like tadpoles), reptiles hatched as tiny versions of the adults, immediately scuttling around and feeding in the same way as their parents.

Hylonomus

Eryops

SEA, MORE OR LESS

The quantity of water on Earth stays the same, but the sea level rises and falls with the temperature. When Earth is cool, sea levels fall as a lot of water is locked up in polar ice caps and glaciers. When Earth is warmer, less water is locked away. The seas are deeper, and flood low-lying land.

Draining the swamp

The Carboniferous period started hot and humid 359 million years ago, with an average global temperature of around 20°C (68°F). With lots of oxygen and carbon dioxide in the air, large arthropods and tropical forests thrived. Later, though, the temperature dropped to 12°C (54°F), oxygen and carbon dioxide levels fell, and large ice caps formed at the poles. The rain forests collapsed and the swamps dried. For 30 million years, the planet warmed and cooled and sea levels rose and fell.

MAKING FOSSILS

We know about the plants and animals of the past because some have been turned into fossils. A fossil forms when the chemicals in part of an organism change after its death, so that it becomes like stone.

An animal dies, often in or near water.

Layers of sediment begin to cover the animal's skeleton. Soft parts might decay.

Sediments harden to become rock. Minerals replace the animal's skeleton, making a fossil.

Few and far between

Fossilization needs very specific conditions. Few organisms become fossils, and of those that do, very few are ever found. There must be lots of fossils still buried deep underground, but we only find those that are brought close to the surface by rocks moving, by erosion, or by digging and mining.

The rock erodes and the fossil is exposed.

FISH OF THE MOUNTAINS

Fossils of marine (sea) organisms are often found inland, even on the highest mountains. These fossils formed on the margins of continental plates, under the sea. When the tectonic plates move and combine, these fossils can end up in the middle of the land.

Fossil in a rock

Fossilized footprints

Becoming a fossil

The body parts that form fossils most easily are hard—bones, teeth, claws, horns, and scales. Soft body parts, such as skin, rarely fossilize. Because it's difficult for squishy bodies to become fossils, we know less about soft-bodied animals—including all the earliest animals. Among plants, seeds and woody stems fossilize more readily than soft leaves.

Fossils form when a plant or animal is quickly covered by sediment (such as mud and sand) and water. That can happen if there is a sudden flood or mud slide, or sometimes if an animal falls into the water (or already lives in the water). It has to be buried quickly, before the body is eaten, broken apart, or rots away.

In the right conditions, the pressure of sediment and water above it turn the body parts and the ground into sedimentary rock. The chemicals in the body change or are swapped for other chemicals. The body transforms into a fossil trapped in rock.

Who was here?

Not all fossils are made from body parts. Some show where an organism has been. Trace fossils can preserve footprints, tail drag marks, burrows, and things like the outlines of feathers or the pattern of skin. All of these make impressions (dents) that stay when the sediment hardens. Trace fossils can reveal some of the ways an animal behaved, but don't include its body.

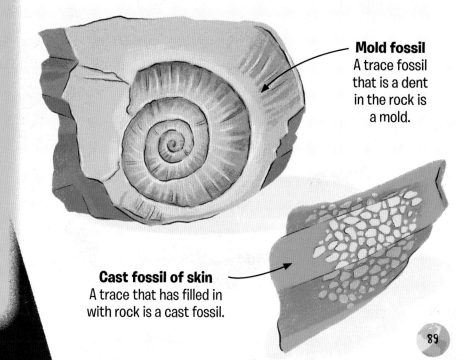

Mold fossil
A trace fossil that is a dent in the rock is a mold.

Cast fossil of skin
A trace that has filled in with rock is a cast fossil.

THE CARBON CYCLE

Carbon dioxide (CO_2) in the atmosphere

Photosynthesis

CO_2 released by plants

CO_2 released by animals

CO_2

CO_2 released by sea life

CO_2 released from soil

CO_2 released by roots

Death and decomposition

Dead organisms and waste products

Carbon locked in fossil fuels

HOW COAL FORMED

Carboniferous trees

Peat

Lignite

TIME

PRESSURE

HEAT

Coal

DEAD WOOD

The first herbivorous (plant-eating) animals did not eat living plants, but fed on plant waste. Arthropods such as woodlice that eat rotting wood remain an important part of the nutrient cycle.

ANIMAL, VEGETABLE, MINERAL

The huge increase in plants and animals on land changed the way Earth's chemicals are recycled. This affected not only the atmosphere, which became suddenly rich in oxygen, but the soil, water, and rocks, too.

Ocean absorbs CO₂

CO₂

Carbon, fast and slow

Early on, carbon was recycled only through rocks and the atmosphere—the slow carbon cycle. The spread of land plants changed that. Huge forests added a second, very rapid carbon cycle. Plants build their bodies using carbon taken from the atmosphere through photosynthesis. When animals eat the plants, they use the carbon in their bodies. Microbes and other decomposers break down the waste of other organisms, releasing carbon to be reused. A carbon atom can be taken from the atmosphere and returned to it in just a few years or even months in this way, while it takes a hundred million years or more to work through the slow carbon cycle. Now, both the fast and slow carbon cycles work alongside each other.

Burning fossil fuels

Coal-fired power station

Fossil fuels

Trees underground

Not all the trees of the Carboniferous forests rotted when they died. Some were covered in sediment in tropical swamps and fossilized. Their carbon lay in the ground for 300 million years. It became the coal we now burn. We are finally returning it to the cycle—but catastrophically quickly.

More cycles

Other chemicals also cycle through animals and plants, including water and nitrogen. Plants and animals both use water to live. They release some as waste, as either liquid or gas. You can see how much water you breathe out by breathing onto a glass and watching the condensation mist its surface. Some water returns to the environment when organisms die. Nitrogen is built into all living cells and released from organic waste by microbes. Different microbes fix the nitrogen from the air into the soil so that it can be used by plants and the animals that eat them.

Lump of coal

WRITTEN IN THE ROCKS

Earth's continental crust is mostly 35–45 km (22–28 mi) thick, but it's not a single, solid layer of rock. Within it are thick and thin layers of different types of rock, laid down over millions of years. The rock varies by place and as the conditions it has been under have changed through time. Later geological activity has tipped, twisted, and folded the layers, making a complex, rich pattern.

Fairy chimneys

Year after year

New rock is laid down on top of old rock. The new rock can be igneous, from volcanoes, or it can be sedimentary. The different shades, textures, and compositions reveal the conditions in which the layers settled. Sedimentary rock sometimes contains fossils or traces of organisms trapped when the sediment collected. When rock layers are undisturbed, the oldest rocks and fossils lie deepest.

Rock strata—straight

What a mix-up!

The oldest rock doesn't always stay at the bottom. Geological activity can move rocks around, disrupting the layers. Patterns in rock show how slabs have been lifted, dropped, twisted, folded, and tilted over time. Veins of different rock or trapped crystals show where rock has been heated up, where molten rock has flowed through harder rock, or where water has carried minerals into rock. Layers of igneous rock show the history of volcanic eruptions.

Rock strata—folded

As rocks are pushed together, the layers of rock can ruck up into folds. Sometimes pressure causes huge slabs to split, and one side falls downward or sideways. Both or either sides might end up tilted. Folds, rifts, and tilting in rocks all tell us what has happened in the past.

Rock strata—tilted

Rock strata —slip fault

Basalt

Tuff

Worn away

Some rocks erode or weather more easily than others. This can make strange features, such as "fairy chimneys." These tall columns are left when the soft volcanic rock tuff erodes, except where it is capped by harder basalt that doesn't erode.

Water easily cuts channels through soft rock like limestone, making underground rivers, caves, and canyons.

WINDING RIVERS

The pattern a river cuts through the landscape reveals the land's past. A meandering river cuts a single path through the land; a braided river splits into lots of different channels, leaving small islands between them. Braided rivers occur where there is a lot of sediment.

Braided river

Meandering river

Mammoth

Pachycephalosaurus

Igneous rock

Dimetrodon

Layers missing in one place might be present in another. The fossils in layers help scientists to date the rocks

Trilobite

All in order

In undisturbed layers of rock, it's easy to see which fossils are oldest—they are buried deepest. Fossils can be put into date order by studying where in the strata they occur. Some organisms only survived for a million years or so. This makes it easy to work out relative dates (which organism is older than another). By comparing rocks and fossils from different areas, geologists can piece together the geological history of the land.

To work out the absolute date (the actual age in years) of a fossil or rock, geologists use radiometric dating. This is based on the rate at which atoms in radioactive elements change

Buried fossils are essentially frozen in time. Until someone digs a fossil out, it is surrounded by rock of the same age as the fossil. In layers of undisturbed rock, we can put fossils in order of date, saying which came before or after another.

Different types of ammonite help geologists date rocks

Finding fossils

Fossils that form on the seabed by the coast often move as the tectonic plates shift and sea levels rise and fall. They might end up buried deep underground, or might be exposed when coastal rock is pushed upward as plates collide. The Burgess Shale fossil bed, now in the Rocky Mountains, contains thousands of fossils from the Cambrian seabed.

Fossils are often exposed when the rock over them erodes, or if a landslip reveals them. Sometimes, fossils from different times are exposed in a cliff or quarry. When people began to build canals and dig more mines in the 1700s, they discovered that different fossils were associated with different layers in the rock.

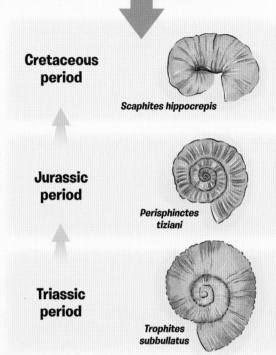

Cretaceous period

Scaphites hippocrepis

Jurassic period

Perisphinctes tiziani

Triassic period

Trophites subbullatus

Fern

Gyroptichius

Igneous rock

over time, which is fixed for each type of atom. From the proportions of changed and unchanged atoms, it's possible to work out a rock's age. Absolute ages change a little as our dating techniques improve, but relative ages don't change: we will never decide that dinosaurs appeared before sponges, for example.

LOOKING AT THE INDEX

Fossils of organisms that were very common but survived for only a short time are often used as index fossils by scientists. Their presence in a layer of rock dates it quite precisely, no matter where in the world the rock is found.

MASS EXTINCTIONS

Conditions on Earth change all the time. When change is slow, organisms can often adapt, evolving different bodies or ways of behaving or moving. But when change is rapid or extreme, many can't adapt quickly enough, and they die out—go extinct. If at least three quarters of all species die out around the same time, scientists identify an extinction event. Mass extinctions completely change the balance of life on Earth.

Pachycephalosaurus

Ornithomimus

Five and counting

There have been at least five mass extinctions in the last 500 million years, largely caused by changes in the climate. Widespread volcanic eruptions, changes in the atmosphere, and even a large asteroid crashing into Earth can cause climate change.

Around 440 million years ago, 86 percent of species died when the temperature and sea level both fell. The rapid development of land plants triggered another mass extinction 364 million years ago, as taking carbon dioxide from the air cooled the planet. The worst mass extinction event was caused by volcanoes, and the most recent by an asteroid strike.

Fast and slow

Most mass extinction events unfold over hundreds of thousands or even millions of years. By contrast, the dinosaurs met their end 65.5 million years ago in a sudden extinction event. It was triggered by an asteroid strike that took just minutes. Its disastrous effects would have taken only a few years to destroy the world of the dinosaurs.

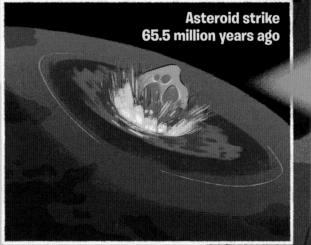

Asteroid strike 65.5 million years ago

Trilobite went extinct about 252 million years ago.

Quetzalcoatlus
went extinct about
65.5 million years ago.

Triceratops

Earth's greatest catastrophe

The largest mass extinction, the "Great Dying," happened 252 million years ago. Massive volcanic eruptions changed the atmosphere and climate, killing 96 percent of Earth's species. The large reptiles that had evolved from the amphibians in the swampy forests were mostly wiped out. It took around 8 million years for life to recover. When it did, smaller, quicker reptiles evolved. They became the first dinosaurs. Another series of extinction events cleared the way for dinosaurs to take over and grow to enormous size.

Parasaurolophus
went extinct about
73 million years ago.

Dodo
went extinct
in 1681.

HERE WE GO AGAIN

We are now at the start of the next extinction event, this time caused by humans. Already, a million species are threatened. The extinction event could be well underway in just a few hundred years.

97

HELLO, HUMANS

In the space opened up by the death of the dinosaurs, mammals rose to take their place. Small mammals first appeared 230 million years ago, but it took a catastrophe for them to take charge. Starting 65 million years ago, they spread over the world, growing larger and more diverse. Humans belong to this group, and to a particular smaller group called primates. From small, squirrel-like animals scampering through the trees, monkeys and apes evolved. Finally, around seven million years ago, the group that would lead to humans separated from the other apes.

Modern humans have been on Earth for just 300,000–200,000 years. In that time, we have changed the path of Earth's story more than any single type of organism since cyanobacteria began to pump out oxygen over two billion years ago.

SLASH AND BURN

Humans evolved as just another animal of the plains and forests of Africa. Just as there are many species of cat, from domestic cats to lions, jaguars and tigers, so there have been many species of human, though we—*Homo sapiens*—are the only remaining species.

Homo erectus

Homo habilis

The human evolutionary story

Seven million years ago, a type of primate produced two different lines of descendants: one became chimpanzees and the other became humans. The first human-type primate, **Australopithecus afarensis**, evolved around three million years ago. The first **Homo** species, called **Homo habilis**, appeared around 2.3 million years ago and made simple stone tools. More advances came with **Homo erectus**, around 2 million years ago. They made better stone tools, learned to use fire and cook food. Using fire was something no creature had ever done before. Later types of human, including Neanderthals (**Homo neanderthalis**) added more accomplishments: clothing, language, and building. With tools, clothes, fire, and language, humans had arrived—even before the evolution of **Homo sapiens**.

THE NEANDERTHAL IN US

Homo sapiens interbred with Neanderthals. We know this because many Europeans share around two percent of their genetic material with Neanderthals. We have discovered this by testing the remains of Neanderthal bodies.

Early *Homo sapiens*

The path to destruction

After modern humans appeared, other species of human slowly died out. It's not clear why. Did we out-compete other species or wage war on them? Or did they die out for another reason? ***Homo sapiens*** spread out of Africa and around the world, first living alongside and breeding with Neanderthals and some others, but eventually replacing them. By 40,000 years ago, the others were all gone.

Humans began to change the world right from the start. Using wooden spears, they could kill large animals—and they did. Large animals died out in all the areas humans entered. Between 50,000 and 3,000 years ago, half the species of large animals went extinct. Humans cleared land to live on using fire. Wearing clothes, they could venture into areas too cold for them in their naked state. With language, they could work together to make even greater changes.

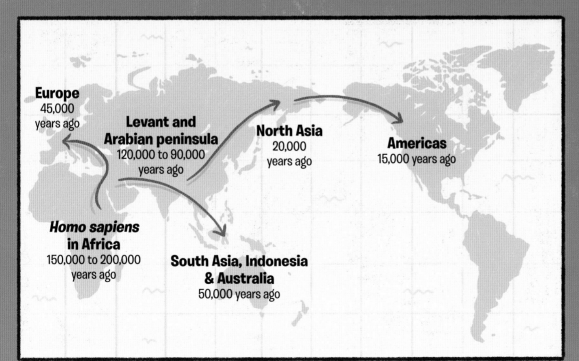

Europe
45,000 years ago

Levant and Arabian peninsula
120,000 to 90,000 years ago

North Asia
20,000 years ago

Americas
15,000 years ago

***Homo sapiens* in Africa**
150,000 to 200,000 years ago

South Asia, Indonesia & Australia
50,000 years ago

CAPTURING THE LAND

At first, humans roamed the land hunting animals and collecting fruit and seeds. Their numbers were small and they had little impact on the biosphere. But around 11,000 years ago, people took a crucial step toward the modern world, one that would soon lead to a far greater impact on the environment and other species.

People probably farmed animals before they grew crops

Home on the farm

Instead of following prey animals and edible plants, people began to settle into communities. They made permanent shelters and farmed the land, keeping and domesticating animals and plants.

Farming quickly changed the environment. People began to clear land, cutting down or burning trees. They dug irrigation channels to divert streams and rivers to water their crops. They captured and kept animals such as goats, sheep, pigs, and cattle. From wolves, they bred dogs to guard their farm animals.

Growing in the greenhouse

This agricultural revolution came at the end of a cold period called the Last Glacial Maximum (often called an "ice age"). Ice covered much of northern Europe and Asia and half of north America. The average worldwide temperature was just 8°C (46°F), while in the twentieth century it was 14°C (57°F). When the ice age ended nearly 12,000 years ago, the level of carbon dioxide in the atmosphere increased and the temperature rose, making it possible to grow crops in many areas of the world. If the world hadn't warmed just then, humankind might not have taken the path it did.

In control of evolution

As soon as humans started to farm plants and animals, they began to change them. By selecting individuals that had the features people wanted, and breeding these together, they directed the evolution of some organisms. They produced animals that made more milk or had more meat, and they grew fruit and vegetables that were tastier, larger, and easier to eat. They did this long before anyone understood genetics and how characteristics of organisms are passed between generations.

THEM AND US

The total mass of a type of organism on the planet is called its biomass. The biomass of land mammals has fallen to one seventh of what it was 50,000 years ago. The biomass of plants has halved. Today, 96 percent of the biomass of land mammals is farm animals—mostly cattle and pigs.

ALL IN THIS TOGETHER

To farm successfully, people need to work together. When it goes well, agriculture produces more food than individuals can grow separately, and more than those doing the farming need to eat. That frees up some people to do other work. With farming established, civilization soon followed.

FEELING SICK

With people living in close proximity to their animals and each other, disease became a problem. Some diseases, such as flu and tuberculosis (TB) crossed from the animals people kept to humans. People packed close together easily spread diseases to one another. As civilizations grew, people began to travel to trade but also to invade and loot other settlements. They moved diseases from one place to another, too.

People working cooperatively could split up tasks, making the group more productive.

Settling down

People needed to stay in the same place to farm the land. They built permanent settlements. These were first just collections of shelters that grew into villages, but later they became towns and cities. The first walled city was Jericho (now in Palestine), founded around 8,500 years ago. It housed 2,500 people. Other cities built up in the Middle East, where areas of fertile ground and a warm climate were good for growing crops and made life fairly easy. A reliable food supply from farms around the cities meant the human population grew quickly. The steady supply of food also freed time for people to do other things. They discovered how to make woven cloth, fine pottery, and even glass. They found metals in the ground that they could work into tools, weapons, and decorative jewels. Writing, organized religion, architecture, engineering, mathematics, and astronomy all began in the area that is now Iraq and Syria. Art, literature, music, and simple technologies made life more enjoyable.

Ancient walled city of Ur

Ishtar gate, city of Babylon

Great wall of China

Cityscapes

The first human homes were probably caves and involved no change to the landscape. Next, small shelters made of branches or piled up rocks would have left little trace and changed nothing. But when people began to build more permanent homes, they had to clear land by cutting down or burning vegetation. They dug the land to make it level and easy to build on. They made bricks from baked clay. They dug ditches and canals to make water flow to and through their cities. They made greater changes than any organism had made before. By changing the surface of the land, humans affected the flow of water over the surface and the habitats of other organisms. They began to shape their Earth.

CHANGING EARTH

Humans changed not only the surface of the land, but the deeper Earth below their feet. With mines and quarries, they sought out metals and minerals from veins in the rocks, brought them to light and combined them in ways that could never have happened naturally.

Neolithic flint mine

Above and below ground

Even with simple tools made of bone, flint and wood, early humans dug out and shaped vast lumps of stone and moved them to areas where they would not normally be found. They used them to make structures that would last thousands of years, such as Stonehenge in England, and pyramids in Egypt and South America.

People also collected metals, at first from the surface. The Ancient Egyptians used iron from meteorites 5,000 years ago. Later they took metals from the rock and from underground, digging mines and collecting ore (metal-bearing rock), which they heated to remove the metal in a process called smelting. They used the metal to make better tools and weapons.

Early metal smelting

People began to make alloys, mixing metals together in new ways not found in nature. These new metals had different properties from their components. The Bronze Age and then the Iron Age were the next great leaps forward in human technology.

From use to ornament

Use of metals went beyond the strictly useful. Once people had what they needed to survive, they mined precious metals such as gold and silver and gathered and polished gemstones that they used to make ornamental objects.

No natural process would have brought these metals together into large lumps, purified and shaped them. No other organism has ever made such deliberate and lasting physical and chemical changes to Earth's resources.

Building Stonehenge

HUMAN-MADE ROCK

Humans went beyond moving and shaping Earth's rocks. The Romans made concrete from volcanic ash, lime (calcium compounds), and broken bits of rock or brick. Their waterproof concrete has survived 2,000 years so far. They also continued and improved glass-making, begun around 5,600 years ago in the Middle East by melting sand so that it fuses.

The Colosseum in Rome, Italy

BURNING THE PAST

Through quarrying and mining, people changed Earth's surface, but by burning fuels we have changed Earth's atmosphere.

The beginning of burning

When humans first used fire, they burned trees and other plant matter. This released carbon dioxide into the atmosphere on a small scale, and the same trees would have died and released their carbon just a few years later anyway, so it had little impact. A few thousand years ago, people discovered fossil fuels—coal, oil, and related products. These would have far more impact.

First fuels

In Ancient Egypt and Babylon, the tarry residue left by evaporating oil, called bitumen, was used in buildings, mummy-making, and to make ships waterproof, but it wasn't burned. Fossil fuels were first burned in China, where bamboo pipes carried gas into homes for heating and lighting more than 2,000 years ago. The Romans burned oil in portable lamps, too, usually plant oils, such as olive.

Romans burning oil in lamps

Natural bitumen deposit

Cranking up the engines

Around 1760, people in Europe and North America began to mechanize industry, using machinery driven by steam. This has been called the Industrial Revolution. The steam was created by burning coal to heat water. It powered industrial machinery and was soon used to drive trains and ships. People began burning oil and gas (methane), too. As machinery moved away from steam power to electricity, fossil fuels were used in power stations. Now we burn fossil fuels in our vehicles, to make electricity, to heat our homes, and to run our industries.

Burnt out

Burning fossil fuels frees carbon that has been buried for up to 350 million years. We have now released millions of years' worth of carbon trapped in coal, oil, and gas in just 250 years—most of it in the last 50 years. At the same time, we have cut down more and more forests that could be locking away carbon in their wood. Carbon dioxide has pushed up the temperature of the planet by 1°C (1.8°F) in 150 years. It might seem a gradual rise, but in geological terms it is super-fast. Heating changes the weather, currents in the oceans and even the sea level.

OIL AND GAS

While coal is fossilized wood, oil is made from the tiny bodies of marine microorganisms squashed under heat and great pressure. Oil deposits deep underground often release gas (methane), which is trapped in the rock above.

Egyptians used bitumen for mummy-making

NEW MOLECULES FOR OLD

Plastic littering the oceans

On Earth and elsewhere in the universe, atoms combine to form molecules in appropriate conditions. Some compounds will only form at a high pressure or temperature, or when other chemicals are present that encourage a reaction. Humans have created conditions that would never occur naturally on Earth, bringing together chemicals to make entirely new materials.

Breakdown of plastic by bacteria

Sticking around

The organic chemicals that make up the bodies of living organisms are broken down when organisms die. Microbes have evolved that can dismantle and recycle them. Some new substances we have made don't decay naturally. Materials such as the hard plastics used in chairs, the polystyrene foam used in drink cups and packaging, fabrics like fleece and lycra, and the plastic film on your snack, aren't broken down. They have not been around long enough for decomposers to evolve to break them down. These could last for thousands or even millions of years, breaking into ever smaller pieces. The smallest pieces are called microplastics.

As we use more and more of these materials, they are piling up in the environment, on the land and in the sea. They affect and endanger wildlife everywhere. Microplastics have been found inside organisms from microbes to whales—and humans. The plastics and other artificial molecules we have made are changing the face of the planet.

HOPE FOR THE FUTURE?

Life adapts and evolves all the time. Some microbes and larger organisms, such as waxworm caterpillars, are evolving to feed on and break down some types of plastic. Better still, some newer plastics are made from plant materials and break down naturally.

Waxworm caterpillar eating a plastic bag

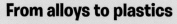

From alloys to plastics

People made alloys by mixing molten metals thousands of years ago. Alloys are a mixture—there is no chemical bond between the atoms of different metals. Experimenting with chemistry, people began to make other materials that are not found naturally on Earth, including compounds such as cement.

More recently, chemistry has given us organic compounds that don't occur in nature. Organic compounds contain carbon and hydrogen. Many of these new compounds are polymers—molecules made of long chains of repeating patterns of atoms. Plastics are all organic polymers. Most are made from oil.

WREAKING HAVOC

Humans have changed planet Earth beyond recognition in just over 10,000 years. We must now learn to keep our influence in check. We must act differently to prevent dangerous global heating and mass extinction.

EMPTY LAND

Indigenous Americans lived alongside the wildlife of North America for thousands of years, but colonists disrupted the balance. The Plains were once home to huge herds of bison. Over a period of just 20 years, in 1870–1890, white Americans slaughtered them, cutting the population from 11 million to only 500.

Getting hotter

Burning fossil fuels is not the only way we add greenhouse gases to the atmosphere. Cattle farmed for beef and milk produce a great deal of methane, too. Together, carbon dioxide and methane are pushing up the temperature. In a hotter world, ice caps and glaciers will melt, the extra water raising the sea level and flooding low-lying areas. Heating also changes the weather, bringing more extreme events such as hurricanes and floods. Some places will become too hot and dry for many organisms to survive, or for people to live and farm in.

Family of Orangutans

Deforestation is destoying natural habitats.

Pollinator: bee

Our chemical pesticides kill insects, including many we depend upon for our crops to grow.

Unexpected consequences

The biosphere is a complex web of organisms that depend on one another. Changing one part has knock-on effects. In the 1930s, vast areas of farmland in North America were devastated by drought and dust storms. Farmers had replaced prairie grass with huge fields of wheat. While grass holds the soil in place, wheat has shallow roots and does not. In dry conditions, the wind whisked away the soil, leaving the land unusable.

In the 1950s, over-use of pesticides in the USA killed not just insects that damaged crops, but helpful insects, and predators that eat insects. A drive in China in 1958 to kill sparrows that ate crops led to a plague of insects that would normally have been eaten by sparrows. These disasters reveal how complex and fragile the web of life is.

Killing times

On land, habitat destruction, pesticide use and pollution have killed wildlife, including Indonesian orangutans. Farming replaces a rich ecosystem with one or two farmed species. In the seas, we have over-fished many species, leaving dead zones where hardly anything lives. Coral reefs are destroyed, broken by fishing boats and stressed by hotter and more acidic seas. All of this reduces biodiversity. A diverse biosphere is strong and resilient; lack of diversity makes the whole living system more vulnerable. Scientists believe we are at the start of a sixth mass extinction event—one that we have caused ourselves.

Dust storms in 1930s' America destroyed the land as well as making the air unbreathable.

Healthy coral

Coral in hot or acidic seas lose their helpful algae and turn white.

Bleached coral

THE VIEW FROM SPACE

Humans are now looking to space, both to explore it and to seek other life forms elsewhere. What if those other life forms are looking in our direction? What would they see? What does our planet look like from space?

Signs of life

One of the ways space scientists search for signs of life elsewhere is to look for "biosignatures." These are chemical traces that suggest life is present. Aliens looking at Earth could have spotted these long before humans came along. Billions of years ago, the combination of methane, nitrogen, water, and carbon dioxide would have alerted curious aliens. These gases should react to remove all the methane in a few years. On Earth, microbes were replacing the methane.

The evolution of land plants around 400 million years ago then added an unlikely amount of oxygen to the atmosphere. Oxygen reacts easily with other substances and would be quickly removed unless it was replaced by plants. On some far-off planet, aliens could have tracked the emergence of microbial life, and then the growth of plants.

LEAVING EARTH

Humans are the first species on Earth to leave the planet and travel into space. So far, no one has gone beyond the Moon, but we have sent space probes (craft with no crew) around the solar system. We have even sent two craft—*Voyagers I and II*—beyond the solar system, carrying messages for any aliens that might find them.

Making our mark

Much more recently, the levels of carbon dioxide have begun to vary in a yearly pattern. There is more carbon dioxide during the months of winter in the northern half of the world. That's because most people live in the north, and they use more fossil fuel in winter. It's unlikely that a planet would have such an annual pattern of changing gas unless something living lay behind it.

Broadcast to the universe

Even our radio signals might be spotted leaking out into space. Any aliens with radio equipment less than 100 light years from Earth might pick up signals that are clearly not naturally created. With the right kind of very advanced telescope—one we don't have yet, but are working on—they might even be able to look closely enough to make out our continents and see the heat spots of our cities.

VIEW FROM THE FUTURE

Can humankind stop harming the planet and fix the damage we have done before it is too late for us and the organisms with which we share our world? We still have time, but we need to act quickly and work together.

Making changes

It's easily possible to use wind, solar, and wave power for energy in place of fossil fuels. We can also use heat from underground. These are sustainable energy sources that don't add carbon dioxide or pollution to the atmosphere.

If people ate less meat we could use land more thoughtfully, leaving more available for wildlife. Meat farming produces a lot of greenhouse gas. We can easily feed the world without damaging the planet if we make plants a more important part of our diet.

We need to cut the toxic waste we produce and keep the air, land, and water much cleaner. Our throw-away culture is less than 100 years old—people have lived for thousands of years without disposable packaging and replacing their phone every year, so it can be done.

AVOIDABLE DESOLATE FUTURE?

Back from the brink

The worldwide lockdowns of 2020 and 2021 during the Covid-19 pandemic revealed how quickly the air can become cleaner and wildlife can flourish when we slow down industry and transport. By using resources carefully, using renewable energy, and protecting natural habitats, we can reverse the destruction. We can still slow or stop the global heating that threatens to make parts of the world uninhabitable. We can save the organisms we depend on and live alongside. It's worth making the effort so that we, humankind, remain part of the story of Earth long into the future.

Solar panels

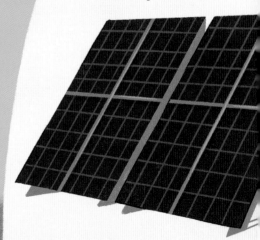

Only one Earth

Humans are using natural resources too quickly. A sustainable lifestyle is one where we use the resources Earth has and no more. Some people use far more resources than this. If everybody in the world used the resources that an average person in the USA does, we would need four Earths in order to support them. The average lifestyle of a person in the United Arab Emirates needs around five-and-a-half Earths, and a typical European takes two-and-a-half planets. On the other hand, if everybody lived the lifestyle of an average person from India, we would only need around half an Earth. It would be hard for people to give up the lifestyles they have become used to, but many aspects of those lifestyles could be preserved if we just changed the way we do things. It is possible to live within our means, and many people do.

A MORE SUSTAINABLE FUTURE?

Wind turbine

GEOLOGICAL AGES

Earth scientists divide our planet's history into different stages in a system called the geological time scale. It is split first into four eons. These are subdivided into eras, then periods, then epochs, and, finally, ages. The division is based on changes in the rocks, which tell us about different conditions and processes on Earth when they were laid down. The eon we now live in, the Phanerozoic, covers the last 541 million years—almost the whole time that complex life has been on Earth.

The geological ages began as a system of relative dates, showing the sequence of Earth's geological history, but they have now been given absolute dates.

Eon	Era	Period		Epoch	
					← Today
Phanerozoic	Cenozoic	Quaternary		Holocene	
				Pleistocene	
		Neogene		Pliocene	
				Miocene	
		Paleogene		Oligocene	
				Eocene	
				Paleocene	
	Mesozoic	Cretaceous		–	← 66–65.5 mya
		Jurassic		–	
		Triassic		–	
	Paleozoic	Permian		–	← 252 mya
		Carboniferous*	Pennsylvanian	–	
			Mississippian	–	
		Devonian		–	
		Silurian		–	
		Ordovician		–	
		Cambrian		–	
Proterozoic	Neoproterozoic	Ediacaran		–	← 541 mya
		Cryogenian		–	
		Tonian		–	
	Mesoproterozoic	–		–	← 850 mya
	Paleoproterozoic	–		–	← 1.78 bya
Archean	–	–		–	← 2.42 bya
Hadean	–	–		–	← 4.0 bya
					← 4.54 bya

(*The Carboniferous is divided into two separate eras in the USA.)

The divisions in the Phanerozoic are based on fossils, but there are few earlier fossils.
The Paleozoic fossils used for dating rocks are mostly trilobites.

TIMELINE 1: EARTH GETS GOING

The universe comes into being with the Big Bang. It started as an infinitely tiny, hot, and dense point. It immediately expands.

Our galaxy, the Milky Way, starts to form.

Earth and the other rocky planets form, as chunks of rock and dust in orbit around the Sun come together.

The first stars begin to pour out light, heat and other electromagnetic radiation.

The first matter to appear is hydrogen and helium.

Supernovas mark the death of early stars, pouring the other chemical elements into space.

The Sun and our solar system start to form.

BIG BANG			HADEAN	
13.8 billion years ago	13.7 billion years ago	13.4 billion years ago	4.6 billion years ago	4.55 billion years ago

120

The small planet Theia smashes into early Earth, a collision that destroys Theia and melts large parts of Earth. The Moon forms from the debris.

The surfaces of Earth and the Moon cool and harden.

Earth continues to be hit by asteroids, delivering extra material.

Water escapes from the magma and forms clouds, then rain. When the surface is cool enough, the rain collects as an ocean.

Some chemicals form pouches or pockets containing other, self-replicating chemicals—a step toward life.

The first microorganisms develop in the water.

The oldest surviving rock has formed.

Earth has its magnetic field.

End of Hadean   ARCHAEAN

4.5 billion years ago

4.5–4.4 billion years ago

4.4–3.8 billion years ago

3.8 billion years ago

Photosynthesis adds oxygen to the atmosphere in the Great Oxygenation Event, causing a mass extinction of anaerobic microbes. Oxygen leaves rust stripes in the rocks.

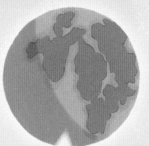

Most land is grouped together as the supercontinent Rodinia.

Photosynthesizing cyanobacteria evolve in the oceans and begin to release oxygen.

The supercontinent Columbia (or Nuna) has most of Earth's land; it is the longest lasting supercontinent.

Falling carbon dioxide levels cool the planet. In a series of Snowball Earth events, temperatures plunge and Earth is covered in ice.

Red algae called **Bangiomorpha** are the first true multicellular organisms that reproduce sexually. Sexual reproduction allows evolution to work more quickly.

Most of Earth's land is grouped in the supercontinent Kenorland.

End of Archaean		**PROTEROZOIC**				
2.7 billion years ago	2.5 billion years ago	2.5–2.2 billion years ago	2.4–2.1 billion years ago	2.1–1.4 billion years ago	1.2 billion years ago	1.1 billion–700 million years ago

An ozone layer begins to form in the atmosphere, making shallow water habitable.

A mass extinction event, perhaps caused by cold, wiped out the characteristic Ediacaran organisms.

The Appalachians begin to form.

The Cambrian Explosion saw rapid diversity in life, establishing all the major groups of animals now living.

Small, sponge-like animals leave the first animal fossils.

The seabed is alive with strange, quilted Ediacaran organisms that leave soft-bodied fossils.

The ozone layer becomes thick enough to make the land safe for life; plants and animals move onto the shores.

End of Proterozoic

PHANEROZOIC **Paleozoic**

| 650 million years ago | 600 million years ago | 577–542 million years ago | 542 million years ago | 530 million years ago | 480 million years ago | 420 million years ago |

TIMELINE 3: LIFE ON LAND

Hot, swampy forest covers much of Earth's land, pouring oxygen into the air. Giant insects and lumbering amphibians rule the forests.

Reptiles evolve from amphibians. Developing an egg that does not need to be laid in water allows them to spread inland.

A giant asteroid strike and volcanic eruptions cause an extinction event that kills the non-bird dinosaurs.

Massive volcanic eruptions and climate change kill more than 96 percent of species on Earth in the "Great Dying."

Fallen trees fossilize, laying down Earth's coal deposits.

The last supercontinent, Pangea, forms.

The Carboniferous rainforest collapses and is replaced by different habitats and organisms in different areas.

The supercontinent of Pangea starts to break apart.

Rising global temperatures and the widespread growth of new forest lead to mammals becoming larger and more diverse.

Mesozoic → Cenozoic

360 million years ago	335 million years ago	320 million years ago	305 million years ago	252 million years ago	175 million years ago	65.5 million years ago	55 million years ago

India crashes into Eurasia, starting to push up the Himalayas and the Tibetan plateau.

Modern humans evolve.

Last glacial period (ice age).

Humanity's threats to the environment increase catastrophically with rising temperatues, environmental destruction, pollution, and rising extinctions.

Humans build the first cities.

First hominins evolve.

Can we turn back the tide and make a better world for ourselves and all the other organisms on Earth? Building a secure future is up to us.

Humans begin to farm, starting to change the land.

With the start of the Industrial Revolution, pollution and use of fossil fuels increase.

| 50-35 million years ago | 3 million –200,000 years ago | 200,000 years ago | 115,000– 11,700 years ago | 10,000 years ago | 6,000 years ago | 300 years ago | 50 years ago | Now & into the future |

125

GLOSSARY

accretion Build-up of small particles to create a larger body, such as a planet.

ammonite An extinct type of sea creature, rather like a squid that lived in a curved shell.

archaea Early and simple life forms with one cell.

arthropod An animal with a hard, jointed outside and no bones.

asteroid A large rock or mix of rock and ice moving through space.

atmosphere Layer of gas around a planet.

atom Smallest part of matter that can be said to be one of the chemical elements.

bacteria Very small living things with a single cell.

billion 1,000 million (1,000,000,000).

bya Billion years ago.

biodiversity Wide variety of living organisms

biosphere The realm of living things in the structure of Earth—all living plants, animals, fungi, and microorganisms.

carbonate rock Rock that contains compounds of oxygen and carbon.

cell Tiny unit of structure in a living organism. All living organisms are made of cells and contain at least one cell.

climate The long-term pattern of temperature and weather.

compound Chemical made of two or more elements.

condense Move from the gas state to liquid by cooling.

convection Flow of heat by moving particles of matter

core Central portion (of a planet).

craton Lump of rock formed long ago from magma as Earth's surface cooled.

crust Rocky outer surface of Earth.

crustacean Animal with a hard, jointed outside, segmented body, and paired legs that lives in water.

cyanobacteria Single-cell microorganism that photosynthesizes.

debris Leftovers or wreckage after something has been destroyed.

domesticated Tamed and adapted to living with humans.

drought A period of extremely dry weather.

dynamic Constantly moving or changing.

earthquake Violent shaking of the ground that happens when tectonic plates grate together.

electron Tiny subatomic particle with a negative charge that orbits around the atom's nucleus.

element Chemical that is made of only one type of atom and can't be broken down into constituent chemicals.

equator Imaginary line around the middle of Earth at its widest point.

erosion Gradual eating away of rock by physical or chemical processes.

evolution Change and adaptation of organisms over time, usually in responses to changing conditions or challenges in their environment.

extinction Dying out of a type of organism.

fossil Relic or trace of a long-dead organism captured in or turned to stone.

friction Force produced by two objects or surfaces rubbing together, generating heat.

genetic Relating to inherited characteristics.

geologist A scientist who works on and studies the physical components of Earth or other planets (such as air, water, rocks) and processes of the planet's formation and history.

hemisphere Half of the Earth's globe.

hydrosphere The water on Earth (oceans, seas, rivers, lakes, seas, ice caps, glaciers, clouds).

hydrothermal Producing or relating to geologically heated water.

inorganic Carbon cycle The slow recycling of carbon through the rocks and atmosphere.

invertebrate An animal without a backbone.

lava Molten rock (magma) coming from a volcano.

lithosphere The rock that makes up Earth (solid rock and magma).

magma Thick, molten and semi-molten rock that lies below Earth's hard crust.

mantle The thick layer of magma (molten rock) that lies between Earth's crust and its core.

metamorphic rock Rock that has changed form as a result of the action of heat and pressure.

meteorite A rock from space that has fallen to Earth.

microbe, microorganism Very small organism that can be seen only with a microscope.

molecule Two or more atoms bonded together.

mya Million years ago.

neutron Subatomic particle with no charge found in the nucleus of all atoms except hydrogen.

orbit To go around a larger body (such as a planet or star), held in place by gravity.

organic Relating to the processes and chemistry of living things.

organism A living thing.

pesticide A chemical used to kill insects and other creatures considered pests.

photosynthesis The process of making a sugar (glucose) from water and carbon dioxide, using energy from sunlight.

planetesimal An early stage in the formation of a planet when it is already a large body of rock but is not yet its final size.

plateau A flat, usually raised area behind a mountain range.

pressure Force exerted by pushing on or squashing something.

proton Subatomic particle with a positive charge found in the nucleus of all atoms.

radioactivity Release of energy by the atoms of a radioactive substance losing subatomic particles and changing from one element to another.

renewable energy Energy gained from a source that will not run out, such as sunlight or wind.

sediment Fine particles deposited in water, such as sand or mud.

sedimentary rock Rock made by compressing sediment over a long period of time.

silicate rock Rock that contains compounds of silicon and oxygen.

smelting Heating rock that contains metal ore to melt and extract the metal.

solar radiation Energy from the Sun, including heat and light.

solar wind A stream of charged particles coming from the surface of the Sun and pouring into space.

strata Layers of rock.

subduction Pulling of one tectonic plate under another. It is usually an oceanic plate (carrying ocean) dipping beneath a continental plate (carrying land).

sustainable Capable of keeping going without running out.

tectonic plate One of the huge slabs of rock that make up Earth's surface.

toxic Poisonous.

trillion One million million (1,000,000,000,000).

ultraviolet Form of radiation with wavelength shorter than that of visible light; ultraviolet is damaging to living things.

vaporize Change from liquid state to gas.

vertebrate An animal with a backbone.

weathering Gradual breakdown of rock by the action of weather (wind, rain, temperature).

zircon Mineral found in some very ancient rocks.

INDEX

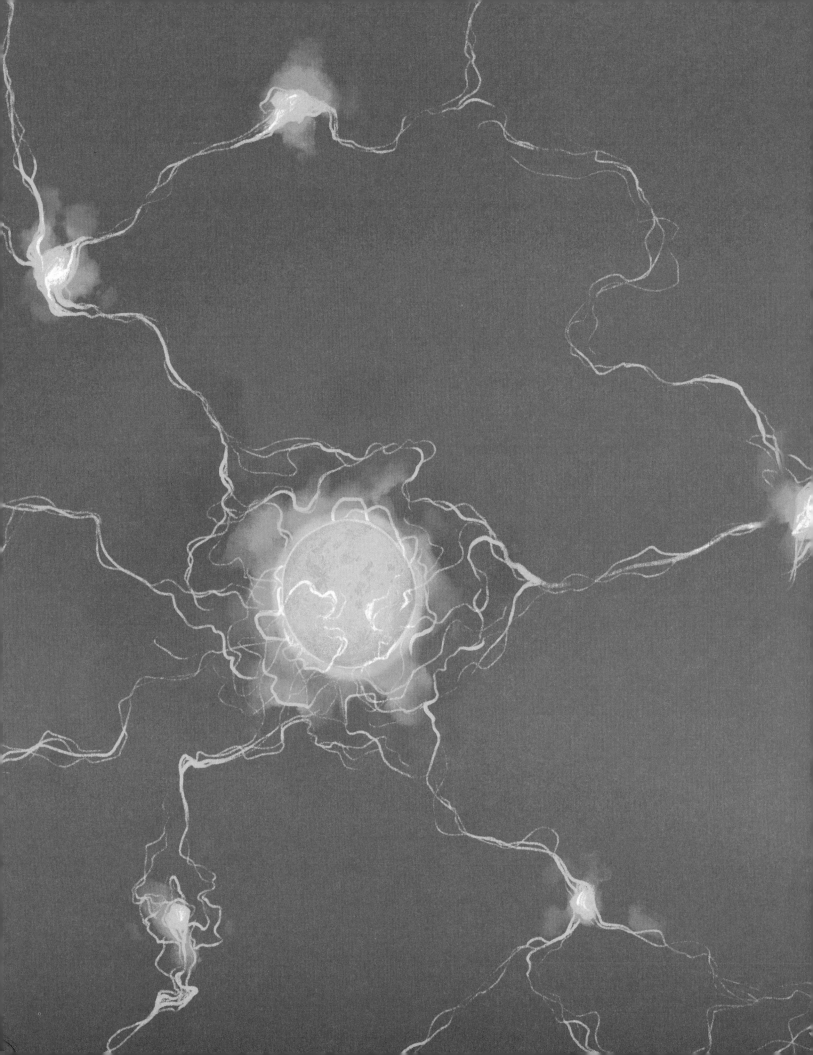